D0603348

PURE STYLE
OUTDOORS

PURE STYLE
OUTDOORS

JANE CUMBERBATCH
with photography by **PIA TRYDE**

RYLAND
PETERS
& SMALL
LONDON NEW YORK

Creative Director **Jacqui Small**

Editorial Director **Anne Ryland**

Art Editor **Penny Stock**

Editor **Zia Mattocks**

Production **Kate Mackillop**

Stylist **Jane Cumberbatch**

Assistant Stylist **Fiona Craig-McFeely**

Assistant Stylist **Alice Douglas**

Printed in China

10 9 8 7 6 5 4 3 2 1

First published in the United States in 1998.
This new edition published in 2002 in the United States by Ryland Peters & Small, Inc.
519 Broadway
5th Floor
New York NY 10012

www.rylandpeters.com

Library of Congress Cataloging-in-Publication Data is available on request.

Contents

PURE STYLE OUTDOORS: NEW IDEAS FOR SIMPLE, STYLISH OUTDOOR LIVING.

INTRODUCTION

Pure Style Outdoors is not a gardening book packed with daunting Latin names, impossible planting schemes, trendy plant varieties, and grand ideas for garden furniture. It is about making the best of your outside space—however small—whether it is a balcony, a vegetable patch, or a backyard. *Pure Style Outdoors* is about being practical, using functional but pleasing tools in a stylish, simple way, and looking at resourceful solutions for making your outdoor area as colorful, textural, sensuous, and as comfortable and welcoming as any room inside your home.

Pure Style Outdoors is about color: the shades that appear in nature, such as sky blues, rose pinks, sunflower yellows, and cabbage greens, and the decorative ideas that will work well with these natural elements, like soft white cotton canvas, mint-green painted trellises, or terra-cotta colored walls. It looks at the many surfaces and textures—both natural and artificial—that work together to make the outdoors a living, organic space, such as blistered, peeling paintwork on doors and walls; old rusting metal furniture and shiny clean tools; earthy, weathered flowerpots; and mossy, worn red brick paving stones. *Pure Style Outdoors* is about being practical and adopting vernacular styles for everything from fencing to garden tools. There are loads of ideas for planting rows of vibrant dahlias, climbing roses, clematis, and morning glories; towering foxgloves and delphiniums; pots or beds of basil, rosemary, thyme, and mint; and edible produce like tomatoes, zucchini, beans, and lettuce. Most plants are quite ordinary, yet they are either beautiful to look at or delicious to eat; and they are all possible to grow from readily available seeds, tubers, or young seedlings.

PURE STYLE OUTDOORS

is also about experiencing the obvious, simple pleasures in life (the very elements that many of us neglect in the hurly-burly of daily living), such as cooking with homegrown herbs, cutting your own roses for the table, or the sheer peace of sitting outside on a warm starry night. It looks at being self-sufficient, with ideas for creating a utilitarian vegetable patch for growing healthy produce—an increasing trend among people who are tired of consuming tasteless vegetables and fruit from supermarkets. *Pure Style Outdoors* also focuses on the decorative aspects of open-air living and the elements required to make your outside area more like a room, and it is full of inspiring ideas for good-value, durable fabrics; simple outdoor furniture and accessories; and basic but good-looking tableware. It is also about eating, with suggestions for delicious outdoor food, using uncomplicated, high-quality ingredients, from pasta with homemade tomato sauce to grilled vegetables and delicious treats for dessert. Finally, *Pure Style Outdoors* shows you how to appreciate the sensuous qualities of the natural elements that make your outside space a living, breathing place—water, light and shade, scent and texture—whether it is the cool, refreshing atmosphere of a wet backyard after rain or the feel of soft, lush grass underfoot.

ELEMEN

TS

Bring life to your outside space with organic textures and color. Be practical and invest in hardwearing old-fashioned tools that do the job properly. Take inspiration from vernacular styles for decorative and functional detailing. Choose colorful flowers that are easy to grow. And use fabrics and furniture to make your outside area a truly luxurious place.

Color

Colors change endlessly according to the seasons, the weather, and the time of day. Strong sunlight on white walls dazzles the eyes with a harshness that makes us reach for a pair of sunglasses, whereas a dull day actually intensifies colors so they appear to leap out of the grayness. Consider color in every aspect of outside living: plants, architectural details, furniture, fabrics, and food. There is beauty in the simplest elements: a climbing white rose; green peas and beans growing in a vegetable patch; and a shady table laid with a crisp white cloth and bowls of green salad. Simple color schemes for plants look distinctive, such as rows of brilliant yellow sunflowers; a white wall covered with tumbling tendrils of sky blue morning glory; or a windowbox painted pale green and planted with hedges of dwarf lavender. Enhance a sense of greenery by painting doors and windows in garden greens. Take note of vernacular styles, such as the colors of blinds and shutters in Latin American villages or the shades of green paint on sheds and fences on farms. Make your outside space more like a room by incorporating colorful throws, pillows, and awnings: try classic shades of white or blue or bold combinations like vivid orange and pink.

White

Whitewash

Stone

Canvas

Pebble

The simplicity of white makes it a purist's dream color and a versatile tool: white flowers can be used as a foil for greenery and white garden accessories look crisp. Although I am tempted to grow flowers in all my favorite colors, I stick to mainly white because the look is very soothing to the urban eye. Each spring I look forward to the sweet-smelling white flowers that bloom on the climbing *Rosa* 'Madame Alfred Carrière', an old-fashioned rose that thrives in its shady environment. White *Clematis montana* produces hundreds of star-like flowers that spread in May along the rails of my roof terrace. Perfect for shady spots is the less-rampant *C.* 'Henryi', which produces huge white flowers during the summer and has even bloomed in a warm December.

Spiky foxgloves are good for height and attract bees, but most are biennial. For stylish, almost instant, windowbox material, I buy pots of white asters, available from nurseries at the beginning of summer. Whitewashed walls are the vernacular style on sun-drenched southern patios, and the look is easy to create with white exterior paint. I use white latex to transform everything from flowerpots to trellis; when it looks grubby or worn, I simply repaint it, although old chairs and tables with blistered, peeling paint can look charming. Hardly a practical choice, but white pillows and cloths look wonderful outside and create an airy, summery feel. I use old sheets for tablecloths and prewashed cotton canvas for pillows and awnings, so at least the whole shebang can be revived by laundering.

Blue

Blue, the color of the ocean and sky and flowers like bluebonnets, agapanthus, and delphiniums, combines well with pink, white, or yellow. As a single color it looks dramatic: a wall covered with jewellike morning glory blooms, a fence bordered with bachelor's buttons, or a bank of papery irises. Sheds and windowboxes look jaunty painted in the bright, breezy shades seen in all oceanside towns. Look to Aegean villages for inspiration and create a rich ocean blue for tubs and flowerpots by mixing a few drops of blue universal stainer into a can of white latex paint. A whitewashed patio looks fabulous with blue and white cotton pillows and tablecloths, while practical, inexpensive bright blue plastic cloths and plates look cheery.

BLUE

Cloud

Bluebonnet

Ocean

Berry

Green

The array of greens in a vegetable patch illustrates the vast spectrum of shades: purplish green cabbages, lime green lettuces, and glossy peas packed in their pods. However commonplace, there is beauty in silvery green lavender, shiny rosemary, lime green alchemilla, and a stretch of lush lawn. In spring, young leaves are luminous and bright with a yellow hue, and as the season progresses they darken to richer shades of green. Potting shed greens, which blend unobtrusively with their surroundings, are the

shades devised by generations of gardeners who have painted fences, sheds, doors, benches, and chairs in these basic hues. Even if foliage is sparse, you can create an illusion of greenery by painting a bench, table, chair, or door in anything from rich olive to paler leafy tones. Sea green or mint shades are more modern and have a Mediterranean feel; they look stylish against galvanized metal buckets and pink- and lavender-colored flowers. Green-and-white striped canvas is useful for deck chairs and awnings, and is the sort of utilitarian material that is still found in traditional fabric outlets.

Pink

Pink is a classic garden color, and photographs of glorious pink and lavender borders of delphiniums, roses, sweet peas, foxgloves, and peonies are what we hanker after and pour over in glossy garden books—the images would be complete with ourselves in appropriate gardening attire (a big floppy straw hat, with shears and an old basket). Nature has so exquisitely matched pink with green: think of spiky lavender heads on trim silvery green stems or fuchsia foxglove bells on lime green stalks. I love to see a trellis with pink rambling roses or a garden wall flanked by towering pink hollyhocks. Fluffy purplish allium balls are excellent for creating height, and

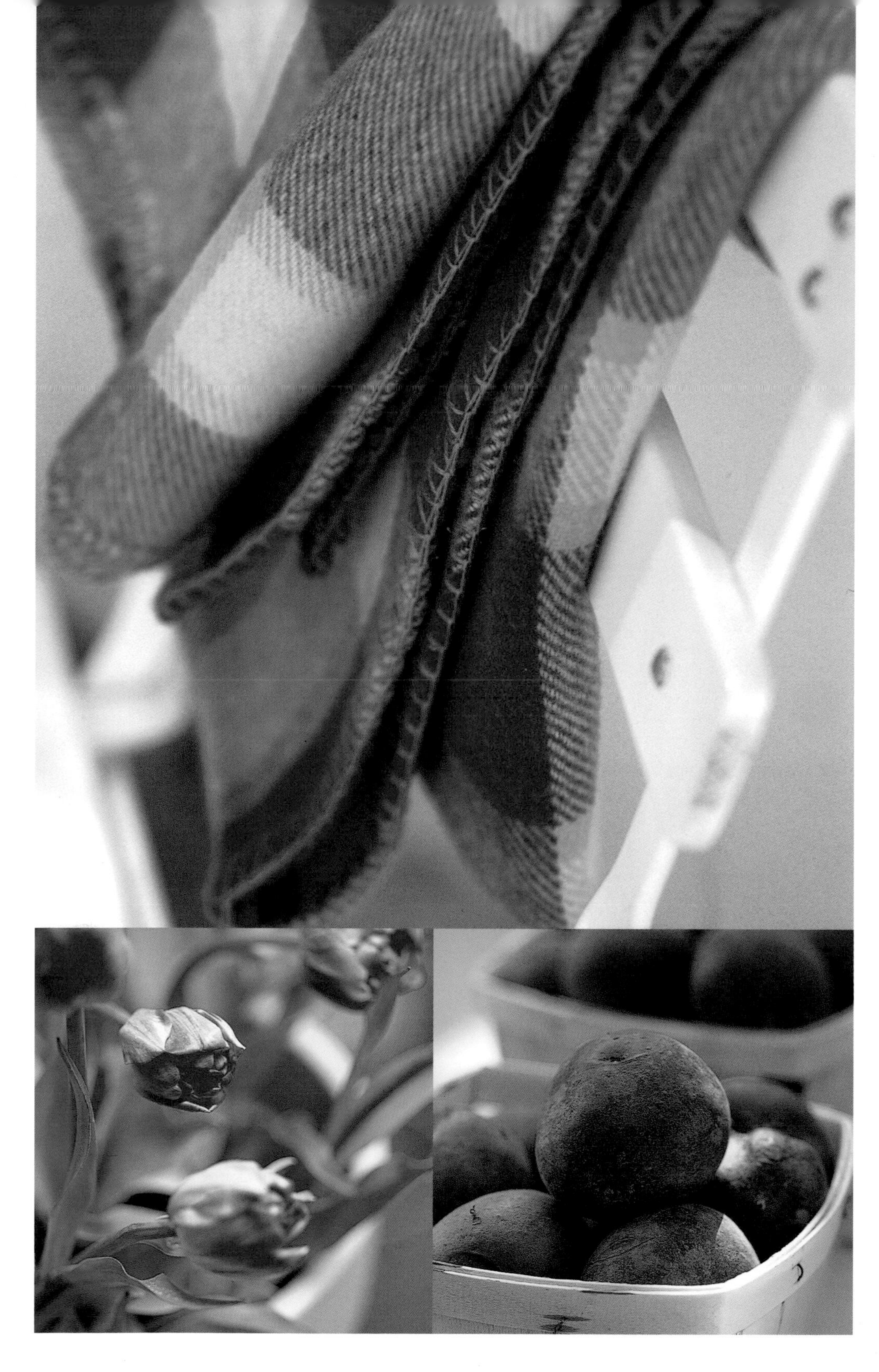

clusters of pinks make pretty and old-fashioned edging borders. Pink is a fabulous color for summer table settings. I have a cloth and chair covers in an old Laura Ashley cotton Provençal print, which look particularly vibrant. Pink and orange checked napkins on liven a white cloth, and lime green napkins look great with fuchsia place-mats and pitchers of alchemilla and pink roses. To complete the effect, serve tasty pink desserts like raspberry gelatin embedded with fruit, or homemade strawberry ice cream.

Orange

Earth

Tomato

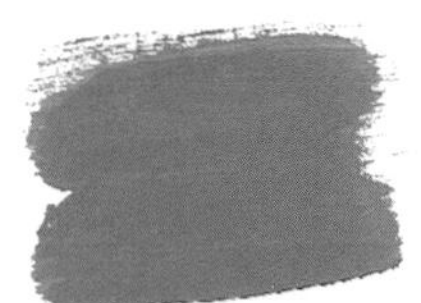

Pumpkin

Terra-cotta

Many gardeners are reluctant to use bold orange flowers, which make a striking, sometimes garish, statement. But although splashes of orange would be unwelcome in a classic country-garden border of pink, lavender, and white, it is a wonderful, daring hot color that can add vibrancy and life to an outside space. Borders of marigolds in a vegetable garden look pleasing and deter caterpillars and snails, and pots of tall orange day lilies look good on a balcony or terrace. Orange and pink are an exciting combination—try modern hybrid orange roses with old-fashioned pinks and cerises, and there are rich orange and pink varieties of dahlias, until recently considered rather kitsch. Dahlias are beautiful, but need to be grown in an orderly fashion, say as part of a vegetable plot, and the cut flowers look wonderful in a simple jar. I vowed not to have any orange in my almost-white garden, but could not resist seed packs of nasturtiums. They are foolproof to plant in pots and trail up a tent of sticks, producing endless orange, yellow, and scarlet flowers that can be added to salads for nutty flavor and decoration. There is something luxuriant about the neat avenues of trees laden with jewellike oranges in California, Florida, and southern Europe. A bowl of fat oranges, complete with their leaves, looks wonderful on a white cloth, and a white pitcher stuffed with marigolds also creates a vibrant splash of color.

Yellow

Candle

Honeysuckle

Nasturtium

Hay

Reassuring bursts of yellow daffodils, narcissi, and tulips punctuate city parks and gardens and the countryside in spring, confirming that all color has not been drained away during winter. I like to plant pots and windowboxes outside the kitchen with dwarf daffodils and narcissi, which have a wonderful heady scent. As a child I used to plant daffodil bulbs and keep them in a cupboard until spring; it was magic to watch the shoots grow and produce a mass of yellow trumpets. I also have a fascination for sunflowers and cannot believe that they can grow quite so tall and produce such giant glowing heads in so few weeks. Try planting rows of sunflowers to make a natural border or to create shelter from the wind. Other yellow favorites include honeysuckle, which is easy to grow from cuttings and has a scent that intensifies during the evening, and pale hollyhocks, which look regal flanking a front door. For the outside table, yellow and green are a stylish combination. Try broiling zucchini and decorate with edible zucchini flowers—wildly expensive in chic farmer's markets but virtually free if you grow your own. For dessert I serve creamy yellow peaches in simple butter-yellow pottery bowls.

Surfaces

Organic, natural, and synthetic surfaces combine to make the garden a living, breathing space. Nature creates an ever-changing textural picture: consider dry, sun-baked terra-cotta and the same surface after a heavy storm, darkened and glistening with puddles. Many surfaces improve with age and exposure to the elements, such as sun-blistered peeling paint on an old garden table, the bleached silvery gray of a weathered oak chair, or an irregular hand-thrown terra-cotta pot, crumbling with moss and age. For boundaries there are materials as diverse as old red brick, New England-style featherboarding, and simple wood-and-wire or stick fencing. For underfoot, old red brick pavers can be laid in a herringbone pattern to edge borders or make practical pathways in a vegetable plot. Smooth square terra-cotta tiles look distinctive laid in a regular checkerboard pattern, and a line of old worn flagstones creates a simple, useful path. Alternatively, there are cobbles, gravel, and luxurious soft lawn. Water is a sensuous, cooling surface, and merely filling up an old sink or bucket lined with pebbles and shells creates a simple makeshift pool. Sturdy textural fabrics for outdoor use include cotton canvas for awnings and woven cane or rattan for seating.

Texture

Contrasting textures in the garden are surprising and exciting, with tactile elements like rough weatherboarding, blistering paint, balls of hairy twine—useful for a multitude of gardening jobs—and brooms with twiggy bristles. The feel of a rough weathered flower-pot or a bleached wooden basket together with the smooth coolness of metal tools make any garden task a sensuous experience. After pounding city streets, treat tired feet to a soft and springy lawn or a carpet of heady

scented thyme or chamomile. It is satisfying to march down a crunchy gravel path or sunbathe on worn, lichen-encrusted flagstones, while teak decking, a good poolside or terrace material, feels smooth to the touch. No-nonsense coarse canvas is a natural, practical fabric for seat covers and awnings, and acts as a foil to indulgent feather-filled pillows and soft throws for siestas. There are also the textures of a dry garden, such as sun-scorched grass and flaking paint, which contrast with those of damp soil and dripping plants, newly watered or after rain, their leaves laden with drops of water.

Deciding what lies underfoot in your garden space is important in both practical and visual terms. The courtyard at the back of my house in London is laid with old bricks that were found ten years ago in a Cambridgeshire salvage yard. They are a rich red terra-cotta that has weathered enough to look as if they were laid when the house was built nearly

Underfoot

300 years ago. A weekly sweep with a stiff-bristled broom is enough to keep the area pristine, and after very wet spells I hose it down with a mild bleach solution to keep slippery moss at bay. Old creamy yellow flagstones were another option that I considered, but they were more costly to transport and to lay per square yard. Paths create a sense of order and lead the eye in exciting and unexpected directions. I visited a diminutive flower and vegetable garden in New York's Catskill Mountains that is neatly crisscrossed by a series of swept hard-earth pathways, an idea transplanted from the southern states where the owner grew up. A charming enclosed vegetable and herb garden I know of

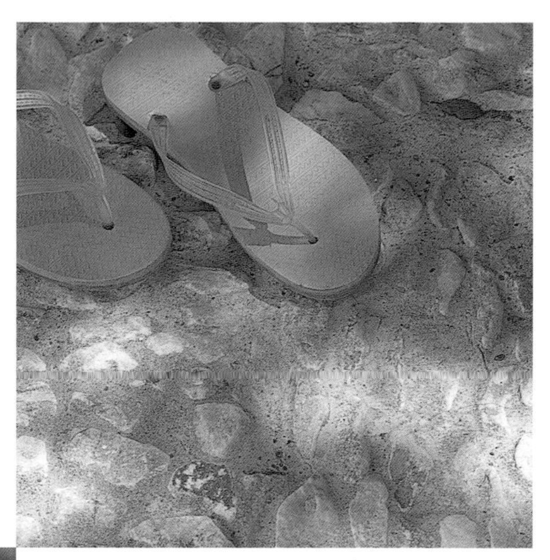

in Connecticut is more formally bisected by uneven brick avenues, while a London vegetable plot belonging to a friend of mine is divided by irregularly shaped slabs of stone. Smooth terra-cotta tiles laid in simple geometric and checkerboard patterns are perfect for hot southern patios. They retain heat and are delicious to walk on barefoot in the cool of the evening. Examples of terra-cotta tiles imported from France, Spain, and Italy usually can be obtained from local suppliers. Or, if you have the time, it is worth looking for tiles salvaged from old farmhouses. The irregularity of a rough and uneven cobbled surface is appealing, and I am inspired by the decorative marble-chip patios and winding alleyways found in many Spanish villages. Other aggregates, such as gravel, create textural, crunchy paths that are practical and reasonably maintenance-free. Specialized suppliers will provide everything from white marble cobblestones and green marble pebbles to beach pebbles, shells, and terra-cotta chips. Teak or pine decking has an oceanside look inspired by boardwalks at the beach and is a useful surface for roof gardens or areas where heavier materials are not suitable. For a greener, softer garden surface, the obvious choice is a velvety lawn. More unusual are flagstones, with herbs like chamomile or thyme planted between the cracks, which smell delicious when they are stepped on.

Boundaries

The earliest gardens were contained for practical reasons—for privacy, to exclude vermin, and simply to enclose a cultivated area of ground. As well as protecting plants from frost, gardens surrounded by walls of red brick feel secretive and romantic. Visit old walled gardens in grounds of historic houses for inspiration for designing your own enclosed area. Also, gather ideas from regional styles for fences and walls when choosing a boundary for your garden or vegetable patch: New England linear picket fencing is charming and can be found in garden centers on both sides of the Atlantic, and flat plank fencing, seen worldwide, can be painted white, garden green, or left unfinished to weather and bleach. Improvised fences of sticks or pieces of curved wattle look rustic and decorative in small vegetable gardens, while a row of espaliered fruit trees or pleached limes and neatly clipped boxwood hedges create natural, green boundaries. To create decorative borders for flowerbeds, try rows of smooth pebbles, lengths of bent or woven wattle, or scalloped Victorian terra-cotta tiles. Another boundary

that should not be overlooked is the facade of the house. Even if the only outside space you have is a window-box, think about the color and texture of the wall around it. A white-painted box planted with white daisies and set against white featherboarding evokes a simple New England cottage, while whitewashed walls will create a Latin

American feel and are ideal for small patios because they reflect light and enhance the sense of space. Climbing roses and honeysuckle look pretty trained up the facade of a brick house. Alternatively, the flat features of modern precast brick walling can be alleviated with paint. The rich barn red that wooden cabins and sheds are painted all over North America and Scandinavia makes a strong backdrop for plants and outdoor furniture. I mixed a greenish blue shade for a stretch of new wall, and this makes a perfect ground for plants or topiary boxwood trees in metal buckets.

Utilitarian gardener

Efficient gardeners are methodical and rigorous about their duties. They rely on good, basic tools and, above all, have a passion for growing things. Sheds, lean-tos, and other covered areas are utilitarian spaces in which to store all their paraphernalia, whether it is a supply of firewood or an array of pots and garden tools. Resourceful individuals cobble together sheets of corrugated metal, salvaged doors, and wood to create makeshift shelters. Then there are glass greenhouses for nurturing delicate seedlings, wintering cuttings, and growing frost-intolerant fruits and vegetables. Gardeners are very fond of sheds, which lurk at the end of many suburban backyards and are stuffed with everything from rubber boots, stakes, seed trays, and tools, to old-fashioned insecticide pumps. Another garden essential is a compost bin, filled with grass cuttings, leaves and other potential mulch. Even a city dweller with little outside space can reserve a corner for organizing gardening gear. Make sure the area is watertight and perhaps construct a lean-to shelter. Paint crates for storing pots, use a side table as a potting bench, build shelves for tools, or screw in hooks for string and raffia. A windowbox gardener might find that a canvas bag does the job.

BODDINGTONS
DRAUGHT

Potting Shed

On a train journey to any large English city, you see patchworks of community gardens, the plots often sandwiched between bus depots and electricity poles. The gardeners who hold the leases are a mixture of knowledgeable old-timers who remember the self-sufficiency practiced by everyone during World War II and a younger generation of gardeners who want their children to know that vegetables come from the earth, not from cello-phane packs. Everyone has a shed, no matter how makeshift or eccentric, and a look inside any might reveal deck chairs; old plastic bottles to up-end on sticks to make improvised scarecrows; string; raffia; yogurt cups for seedlings; and an array of tools. Vegetable patches and mixed gardens need year-round attention, from spring, when bulbs begin flowering and the soil is hoed and fertilized in prepara-tion for planting, through summer, when fruits and vegetables ripen, weeds are battled with, and watering is a constant activity, to fall, when plants are cut back and produce is harvested. These gardens require soil that is fertile, well drained, well tilled,

and weed free. Light and crumbly soil allows air to enter, which sustains the organisms that make up healthy earth; if soil is hard when dry and sticky when wet, dig in as much organic material as you can to lighten it. Inexpensive meters for testing the acidity of soil are available—a pH of 6.5 is ideal for general purposes. With increased popularity in organic growing methods and less reliance on chemical pesticides and fertilizers, many gardeners are keen to make their own humus and grow plants such as marigolds, which are said to destroy snails and caterpillars. Yet it is rather impractical not to resort to manufactured fertilizers if you have restricted growing space. I buy bone meal and apply a weekly dose of all-purpose fertilizer to help my roses, clematis, delphiniums, foxgloves, herbs, lettuces, and tomatoes. I also get bags of well-rotted horse manure from a nearby city farm, which I apply in copious quantities in early summer and fall. If you have space, a compost heap is essential, with ingredients such as teabags, eggshells, vegetable and fruit peels, manure, and grass clippings. Keep it moist with water and turn it occasionally to aerate it.

Structures

There is a fashion for growing anything from nasturtiums and tomatoes to beans and sweet peas up tentlike frames made from stakes or twigs. The effect, inspired by old-fashioned growing methods, is easy to achieve, decorative, and a practical way of training plants. Single sticks of wood set in compact rows are another functional but charming way of training beans and other climbers that do not produce heavy fruits, and rows of thin twiggy sticks are great for training sweet peas. For really simple but effective structures, buy lengths of chicken wire. Alternatively, a simple wooden square trellis, available from any good garden center, looks really stylish painted a shade of garden green: I used it for training clematis over a rather ugly stretch of brick wall on my roof garden. Arbors, arches, and pergolas create shady areas in which to relax, and are also decorative ways of supporting climbing roses and many other brilliant blooms. Simple metal rose arches can be obtained from garden centers or mail-order catalogs, and the rather unsightly black finish that many come in can be covered with tough enamel paint. Pergolas made of sticks are particularly romantic and easy to construct; coat the ends that sit in the earth with an anti-rot preparation. Train a grapevine or other vigorous climber over a structure made of wood or wire and metal to create a shady vine pergola that becomes a little outside room.

Tools

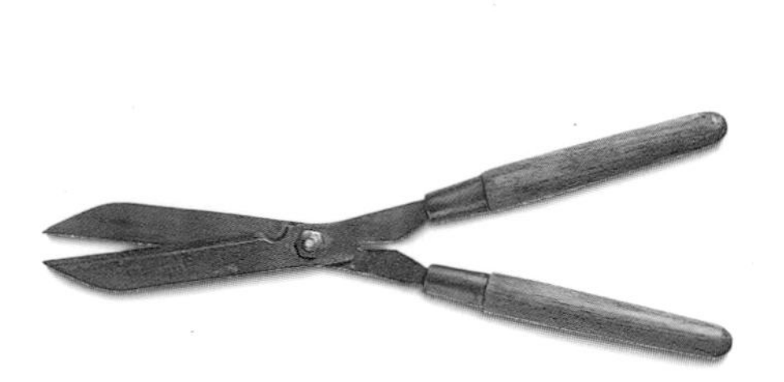

Wooden-handled garden shears for trimming hedges and cutting back shrubs.

A set of all-metal trowel, dibble, and fork—essential tools for potting plants and seedlings—are practical and easy to clean.

Keep a besom broom for sweeping up leaves and twigs, and a supply of cane stakes to build tent supports to train climbing plants.

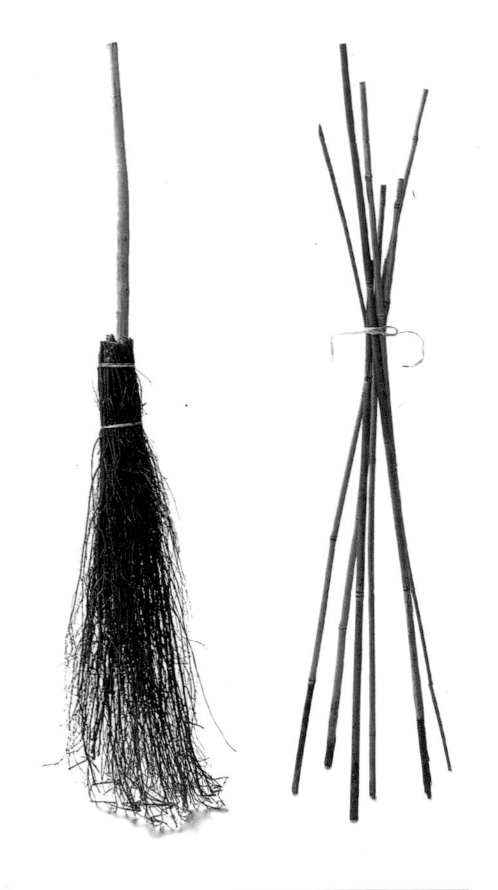

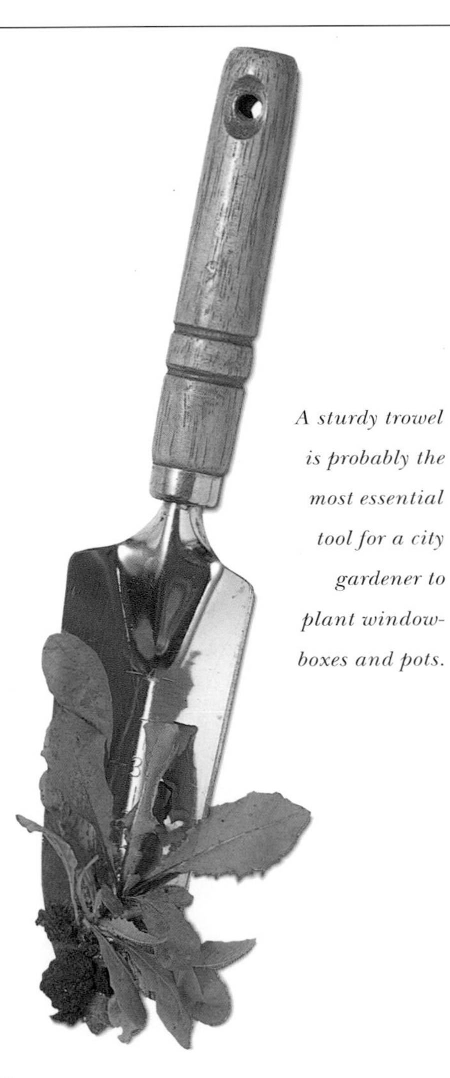

A sturdy trowel is probably the most essential tool for a city gardener to plant window-boxes and pots.

I have a few totally indispensable tools for my gardening activities, which live in the old coal shed—my version of a potting shed. Most of my gardening is carried out in pots and windowboxes, and I use my watering can twice a day in hot weather to satisfy the thirsty demands of the potted plants. Invaluable for pruning are shears and a pair of tough gloves. The essential fork,

This plastic apron is practical gardening attire, as is a pair of tough gloves like these vinyl-coated ones.

Curvy and compact, traditional wooden baskets are perfectly shaped to carry your tools, plants, and other gardening gear.

Bright green trash bags are a jollier alternative to the ubiquitous black garbage sacks.

A big plastic tote like this is inexpensive and can be used to carry everything from picnic gear to logs from the wood shed.

A rake for leaves, a traditional pitchfork, and a solid shovel with a wooden handle are all useful implements for the gardener.

I have several metal watering cans; this galvanized example is good because its boxy proportions make it easy to carry and pour.

trowel, and dibble are normally tucked into a pot. There are also stakes, wire, and string for training new growth, and hats, old shirts, and rubber boots. I also keep cans of latex for painting trellises, pots, and furniture, and plastic bottles of diluted liquid detergent to rid the roses of aphids and more potent insecticide to deal with blackfly that plague the nasturtiums.

Raffia and string are invaluable for all sorts of jobs, from tying tomato plants to stakes to hanging up bundles of bulbs to dry.

Plant labels need not be boring to look at. Metal or wooden garden tags are much more stylish than plastic ones—and they are not expensive.

Rubber boots are the most sensible type of footwear for gardening jobs on soggy wet days—this pair is lined with leather.

Containers

Almost anything will do as a plant container: plastic bowls, old sinks, terra-cotta pots, wooden tubs, and galvanized metal buckets are just some examples. Containers make focal points within a garden and can be moved whenever you feel like it. Try a pair of tubs with standard boxwood or bay trees on either side of a door or mass together terra-cotta pots filled with herbs. Create a miniature garden on a windowsill or balcony with windowboxes containing anything from little lavender hedges to trailing nasturtiums, vegetables, or herbs. Wooden seed trays, picket-fence windowboxes, and twiggy troughs are all useful for displaying pots of herbs, spring bulbs, and summer bedding plants. For added color I like to paint pots green, blue, or white. Good drainage is a key to successful gardening, and normal-size pots with a central hole need only a few stones in the bottom before being filled with soil. For a well-balanced potting medium, use soil that is light, friable, easily drained, and nourishing. Mix heavy soil with sharp sand, and light soil with rich loam. Add granulated peat to help retain the moisture, and fertilizer for nourishment. With regular feeding and the addition of potting soil, potted plants will remain healthy in the same soil for many years.

Terra-cotta

Shapes range from traditional flower-pots to giant Ali-Baba urns. Many garden specialists import wonderful textural terra-cotta pots from Spain, Italy, France, and Mexico. Salvage and reclamation yards are good sources of old hand-thrown flowerpots—I have four or five beautiful, worn examples that came from the glass greenhouses of a big old country mansion. Machine-made terra-cotta pots look uniform and lack the texture and irregularities of hand-thrown examples. To add instant character to cheap pots from garden centers, I mix a wash of white latex paint colored with green, blue, or terra-cotta paint. Pots left out in the elements weather quite quickly, but you can accelerate the process by smearing them with yogurt to encourage the growth of green moss. I use giant terra-cotta pots in all shapes for planting clematis, trailing tomatoes, honeysuckle, and lavender; and rectangular containers alongside a wall for growing taller things like foxgloves and delphiniums. Create a windowsill or balcony kitchen garden with herbs planted in individual pots. Rosemary, parsley, marjoram, rocket, sage, mint,

Ideal for a rooftop or balcony vegetable garden is a long tall flowerpot painted with vibrant lime green latex with a tent of plant stakes and raffia to support a cherry tomato plant.

A pot painted with lime green latex paint and planted with an ornamental halo looks good placed on a windowsill or arranged in a row with three or four others along a terrace wall.

Old terra-cotta bowls look decorative planted with herbs or bedding plants like pansies; make sure there is a hole for drainage.

A shallow terra-cotta planter looks good filled with several low-growing plants such as these baby's tears.

A nineteenth-century-style terra-cotta rhubarb forcer with a removable lid can either be planted with tiny trailing flowers or left empty as a decorative feature.

thyme, and basil (provided it is sunny, warm, and sheltered) grow well with a strict daily watering regime. Or use terra-cotta pots for vegetables: I have attempted lettuces, trailing tomatoes, and dwarf cherry tomatoes with success. For a structured look, ball-shaped boxwood plants look architectural in square pots, and little boxwood or bay standards suit the rounded shapes.

left to right *A conical wall pot painted with a wash of white and terra-cotta latex for a weathered effect; and two tall terra-cotta pots planted with an amaryllis and a topiary boxwood tree.*

Ornamental curly kale planted in a simple galvanized metal container make an unusual decoration for the table or windowsill.

An old powder blue enameled camping dish is ideal for planting violas and other tiny flowering plants.

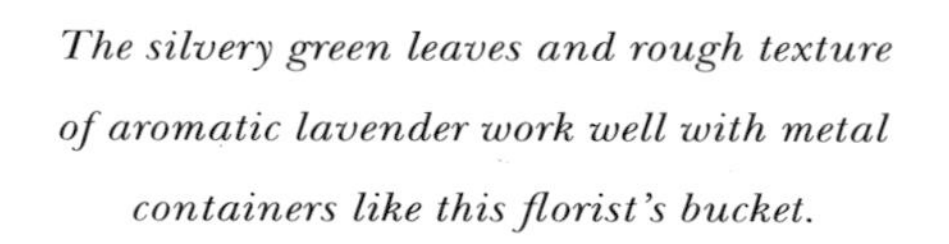

A basic metal tin is ideal for growing wheat grass—the latest organic wonder-root, which can be liquefied to make a nourishing drink.

A weathered metal bucket is a no-nonsense, yet pleasing, container for a boxwood standard.

The silvery green leaves and rough texture of aromatic lavender work well with metal containers like this florist's bucket.

A shapely bay standard in a metal bucket can be placed on a table to create a sense of height.

Metal

Functional and simple galvanized metal equipment and tools for the garden, such as watering cans, metal bins, and corrugated-iron shacks and sheds have a rough, honest appeal and create a foil to the softness of flowers and plants. Metal containers for plants—whether they are buckets, bowls, troughs, or cans—have a modern, utilitarian look that makes a change from traditional stone or terra-cotta containers. The silvery gray color of the metal works well with greenery, and textured galvanized metal surfaces look wonderful contrasted with shiny green rosemary bushes or silvery gray-green lavender leaves. Simple architectural shapes, such as topiary boxwood or bay look smart and stylish in metal buckets, which can be bought inexpensively from hardware stores. You can even recycle baked bean or tomato cans and make them into vases for cut flowers or, with small holes punched in the bottom for drainage, containers for herbs. The Spanish are particularly fond of this idea and use giant olive oil tins or oil drums to plant everything from geraniums to hollyhocks.

Sky blue and sea green plastic pots are an alternative to traditional terra-cotta. Use as a table decoration or display five or six on a sill.

Based on the design of egg boxes, these functional cardboard seed trays made of wood pulp are available at most garden centers.

For a plain, natural effect, fill an unpainted wooden box with silvery rosemary and thyme.

Wood and plastic

For a rustic look, a basic rectangular windowbox in strong hardwood like cedar can be left to weather to a lovely silvery gray or painted to unify doors, walls, and furniture. For a simple, uniform scheme, plant brilliant white or blue hyacinths, hedges of dwarf lavender, nasturtiums, or white asters. A simple windowbox kitchen garden may have herbs like chives and parsley at the back and trailing cherry tomatoes at the front. It is such fun to pick your own juicy tomatoes and to have a few herbs at hand for giving delicious flavor to summer suppers of fish, new potatoes, and salad. Wooden slatted tubs, barrel shaped or square, can be filled with anything from wildflowers and herbs to topiary boxwood trees or giant sunflowers. Pots of herbs in wooden seed trays look good on outdoor tables. Steer clear of plastic pots and windowboxes in soulless colors and shapes. Be inventive and adapt bright blue and green buckets and sink bowls, from a hardware or discount store, for a more contemporary look.

Plain white plastic cups, which can be bought very cheaply at any supermarket, make useful and simple pots for planting young plants and seedlings.

A windowbox with picket fence detail, filled with pots of herbs, is ideal for a kitchen garden.

Basic and traditional wooden seed trays are a practical and innovative way of displaying pots of flowers or herbs.

An old wooden box has been brightened with white latex paint to make a windowbox for flowers or herbs.

An ugly, standard plastic windowbox has been transformed with two coats of powder blue latex paint and then planted with ornamental kale for a contemporary look.

Flowers and plants

It is exciting to grow your own flowers, vegetables, herbs, and fruits—and you do not have to be an expert. It is equally as pleasing to nurture a windowbox or grow rocket from seed as it is to plan a large-scale garden. Color is the most important criterion for me when it comes to choosing plants. My favorites remind me of childhood summers: white climbing roses; fat purple alliums; white and pink-purple clematis; pink foxgloves; deep-blue and lavender delphiniums; blowsy pink peonies; and gaudy orange, pink, white, and red dahlias. I am an impatient gardener who wants the picture on the seed packet to be realized overnight. It is satisfying to take a cutting of a plant like honeysuckle, stick it in the earth, and actually see it start to shoot a few days later. Yet with the constraints of domestic hurly-burly, it is more sensible to invest in pots of young plants from reputable garden centers. When it comes to homegrown produce, it is possible to grow things in confined spaces: I had a good crop of tomatoes this summer from four or five plants in pots on the roof garden, plus nasturtiums and rocket grown from seed. There are also pots of herbs—basil, mint, thyme, and rosemary —just some essentials to have for flavoring everything from fish to salads.

Flowers

I am not a serious gardener because color is my main priority when choosing flowers. I am not concerned with planting fashionable varieties and I probably make dreadful gardening gaffs simply because I want the colors to look right together. I am sure it is not *de rigueur* to mix tomatoes, nasturtiums, and white clematis—a group I had on my roof terrace—but against the dreary urban roofscape of concrete and brick, the bursts of vibrant orange, yellow, scarlet, and white on a backdrop of greenery looked cheery. My dream is for a totally white garden (much like my ideal white minimalist interior), scented, romantic, and flowering all year. To achieve the former, I

need tons more gardening expertise than I am prepared to gain, and with three children the latter, interior, vision is not meant to be—at least not for a few years. Therefore, I am content to be less exacting about color in the garden and to experiment and make mistakes. I stick loosely to a palette of individual colors that also marry well with each other: white, pink, lavender, and hot oranges and yellows. I find that blocks of single colors tend to be more dramatic and less confusing to

opposite, clockwise from top left *Pretty blue border geraniums; leggy delphiniums to add height; delicate white violas; foxgloves—easy to grow, but most are biennial; agapanthus, with ball-shaped flowers on slim green stems.*
above *Not all poppies are red; more delicate shades include white, lavender, and blue.*
right *Passionflowers are vigorous climbers.*

the eye, like a wall smothered with white roses, tubs of green topiary box standards, or a path edged with pinks. For height and drama I love foxgloves, especially white ones. Having disdained this woodland plant for years as a self-seeding weed, gardeners now compete to produce varieties for flower shows in the most subtle shades of pink, white, and lavender. The tag attached to my appropriately named "Albino" describes the majestic spikes of tubular white flowers that bloom during June and July, and, of course, the warning that foxgloves are toxic if eaten. I managed to grow them in large pots on the roof with quite satisfactory results. One day I will plant pots of white agapanthus, whose graceful stems support lacy heads—another good plant for height that grows well in

sunny spots. Delphiniums seem ridiculously easy for amateurs like me to grow, and their tall spikes with a froth of blue and mauve flowers exist quite happily in potting soil enriched regularly with bone meal and plant food. Climbing white roses and pot-grown rambling clematis are other favorites that are good for camouflaging unsightly objects. Passionflower is a pretty climber that grows well in sheltered positions. The blooms last only a day or so, but are produced so freely that there is a constant display from June to September, sometimes followed by edible orange

opposite, clockwise from top left *Peonies look beautiful even after heavy rain; voluptuous, rain-soaked summer roses; morning glory's trumpetlike flowers live less than 24 hours.*

clockwise from top left *Poppies look wonderful in wild, uncut grass; border geraniums add a touch of delicacy; woodland foxgloves are at home in both country and urban gardens.*

fruit. Morning glory is another eager half-hardy annual that produces myriad trumpet-shaped flowers in sky blue, magenta, or deep pink, from June to September. The flowers last only part of a day, normally closing during early afternoon, but shaded from the mid-day sun, they may last until evening. A traditional cottage-garden flower with late-summer blooms, often used to edge a path or vegetable patch, the perennial dahlia is ideally suited to making a brash color statement. With many varieties and marvelous combinations of white, crimson, pink, yellow, and purple—some with two colors in one stem—dahlias are making a comeback in gardening circles. Zinnias are another showy flower in gorgeous orange and pink, with broad flat, rolled, or frilled petals. They flower in late summer and give life to a border. While carnations are deemed rather kitsch, the common garden pink, which is in the same family, is a pretty, feathery, old-fashioned border flower that is easy to grow and maintain.

opposite *Dahlias make bold color statements.* **clockwise from top left** *A fuchsia dog rose; a feathery petaled dahlia; homegrown nasturtiums; pretty cottage-garden pinks; a vibrant zinnia; poppies growing in long grass.*

Herbs

Herbs look beautiful and taste good: chamomile or thyme are fragrant planted between flagstones; parsley, thyme, and mint make good cottage-garden beds; and rosemary or bay can be clipped into architectural shapes. Even if you are restricted to a windowsill or balcony, it is possible to grow in containers most of the herbs needed for cooking. Tomato salads and sauces without basil would be dull, and I generally keep a plant in the warmest, most sheltered spot for the duration of summer and freeze sprigs for use in winter. Sage grows quite happily on the roof terrace and is reasonably hardy. I love the strongly scented leaves chopped sparingly into sauces and salads. Part of the pleasure of growing rosemary is cutting the spikes, which releases the heavenly sharp scent. Used sparingly, rosemary is delicious with pork, chicken, and roasted vegetables. Mint has an irresistible smell and flavor, and grows like wildfire. I use tiny sprigs to decorate ice cream and to add flavor to new potatoes. Lemon balm is useful to add to wine punches and salads and it is a pleasure to pinch the scented leaves.

clockwise from top left *Basil, delicious in salads and sauces, thrives in sheltered spots but is destroyed by the first hint of frost; lavender looks and smells wonderful and can be used to flavor cookies; drought-resistant rosemary is deliciously aromatic but needs to be used sparingly in the kitchen; lemon balm grows vigorously and is delicious in punches; sage keeps its leaves throughout the winter and tastes good in stuffing and stews.*
opposite *Parsely is a versatile herb and is particularly good for flavoring salads.*

Edible flowers

Edible flowers add color and taste to salads, desserts, and cakes. Crystallizing rose petals is a magical way of dressing up cupcakes or buns. Wash your favorite petals from the garden, dip them in a mixture of egg white and sugar, then leave them to dry. Try crystallizing viola, pansy, geranium, and lavender flowers, too. Bonnetlike pansy flowers make shortbreads into edible works of art, and bright orange marigold petals look pretty on top of iced cakes. Bright blue borage flowers, traditionally used in ice-cold lemonade, look pretty on a salad of zucchini and cucumber. Both dandelion and nasturtium flowers and leaves make vibrant additions to green salads, and yellow zucchini flowers are very tasty if you dip them in a light batter and deep-fry them for a few minutes, and they also look good raw in salads.

opposite, top to bottom *Pansies, borage, and crystallized rose petals are pretty decorations for cookies, salads, and cakes.* **far right** *Fresh herbs and flowers.*

right *Broiled zucchini decorated with zucchini flowers; unpicked flowers will become new fruits.* **below** *Nasturtium flowers and leaves taste nutty in salads.*

Produce

I have always had a fascination for seed packets and the magnificent specimens that are promised in the illustrations. Even though we lived in London with little room for a vegetable patch, my parents grew zucchinis, tomatoes, and raspberries covered in bridallike veiling to keep off the birds. We had two big plum trees, one a Victoria that bent double and eventually collapsed with its yield of fat, juicy plums. My mother was endlessly making jelly, and there always came a point when my sister and I never wanted to see a plum again. My family and I are learning to grow things using the knowledge of the villagers near our house in Spain. We have learned how to plant, stake, and care for tomatoes, how to dip the right-size ridges for potatoes, how to take the seeds out of sunflowers, and even how to thresh chickpeas. To cope with a glut of tomatoes, we skin and bottle them to store away for use in winter salads and stews. Even though the slugs and some kind of wilt threatened, we cut and ate our own magnificent cabbages which, lightly steamed with

butter, even the under-eights ate without dissent. At home in England, apple trees provide fruit for cooking and eating, and there are plenty of raspberries, strawberries, and gooseberries to make delicious jelly. I have even been successful on my roof terrace this summer with a trailing variety of tomato that grew up a tent of sticks and produced tasty rosy-red specimens. I have also had luck with rocket, which grows with ease from seed and is a delicious, nutty, and slightly bitter addition to salads. Wild food is especially fun to gather. Blackberries come to mind immediately, and they make wonderful jelly and pies. Sloes found in country hedges are bitter raw, but, added to gin and left to steep for a few months, make a pretty pink, sweet brew in time for Christmas.

Fabrics and furniture

Toughness and durability are essential qualities for outdoor fabrics and furniture. All-purpose cotton canvas is a texture that works well for simple chair covers and shady awnings. Cream muslin—cheap, durable, and washable—is ideal for making tablecloths, slipcovers, and cushions. Another favorite understated fabric is blue-and-white ticking, a robust cotton twill closely woven in narrow stripes. Traditionally used for pillows and mattresses, it looks good in any setting, whether as cushions on a hot whitewashed patio or as simple chair covers on a leafy deck. Plasticized cotton or vinyl make useful waterproof tablecloths and are available by the yard in checks and bold colors at department stores. You do not have to invest in extra sets of furniture for outside: indoor folding chairs can be whisked out when the sun shines, as can a lightweight table. If you prefer permanent outdoor furniture, oil hardwoods regularly or coat with tough exterior paint. The alternative is the aged, weathered effect: peeling, paintwork; algae-encrusted wood; or old rusty metal—organic textures that look at home among outdoor elements. There are plenty of outlets for cheap junky furniture that can be left outdoors, but all expensive pieces should be brought inside once summer is over.

Fabrics

Fabrics need to be tough and hardwearing for outside use. The best choices include canvas, linen, and washable plastics. Department or fabric stores are great sources of striped deck chair canvas, plasticized cottons for cloths, and basic cotton muslin. For stylish colors—bright blue, green, pink, and orange—head to interior design stores that update their collections as regularly as fashion houses. Heavy cotton canvas is one of the most adaptable fabrics and can be used to make sturdy slipcovers for garden chairs. It is important to wash natural-fiber fabrics before cutting and sewing, so you can rejuvenate them in the laundry without disastrous shrinking. I like to buy tough blue-and-white striped or plain cotton canvas to make awnings for my yard. The ends are hemmed and the corners punched with metal eyelets (very easy to do with a hole-punching kit). The awning is secured to hooks on the wall with nylon rope that can be adjusted as necessary. White and cream fabrics look fabulous, especially if your outside space is painted white. Imagine that you are creating the outside version of a simple, minimalist interior. White cotton slipcovers can disguise unmatched chairs, and a plain white sheet flung over a table looks stylish and provides a neutral background for food. Scatter pillows should be filled with feathers, and bench pads should be of good-quality foam and have removable covers secured with Velcro, buttons, or ties. Fabrics in vibrant seaside blues, apple greens, and rosy pinks add color and enhance surrounding flowers and greenery. Pink and orange cloths and napkins look bright and contemporary, while blue-and-white ticking looks good in any setting and makes understated covers for cushions, bolsters, and chairs.

See pages 154–5 for fabric details.

11
12
13
14
15
16
17
18
19
20
21
22
23
24
25
26
27

Furniture

Simple wooden benches of teak or another tough hardwood can be left in their natural state or painted with exterior paint, like this one in bright blue.

This contemporary rocking version of a traditional deck chair folds away for easy storage. It has a lightweight aluminum frame and a tough green synthetic cover.

Picked up in a thrift store, this old metal folding table with blistered paint looks good in the garden all year and can be used to display pots of spring bulbs or laid for summer meals.

Cheap, practical, but totally charmless, molded plastic garden furniture has spread like a rash through parks, hotels, and gardens. Here are some simple, decorative alternatives for seats and tables that combine form and function without breaking the bank. Anything that folds is useful, so it can be brought inside when the elements become inclement. My favorites are small wooden

Solid wooden garden tables with painted surfaces that weather well are one of the most practical outdoor items and can be put to use at any time of year.

A small folding table is a perfect dining table for one person and two or three can be put together to accommodate more people.

A folding director's chair, with a yellow checked cotton seat and back, is painted a sludgy gray that blends with garden greenery.

A flat-pack pine potting bench has been updated with coats of sea blue latex. Use it to store flowerpots, seed trays, and tools, or as a serving table for food.

A traditional deck chair in a tough blue-and-white checked cotton cover looks crisp and cheerful in any outdoor setting.

A cheap wood-and-fiberboard folding table that seats eight people comfortably can be carried outside and dolled up with a cloth in white cotton or bright lime green vinyl.

Lightweight folding chairs are stylish for outdoor dining. They come in lots of colors and old ones are often nicely worn and have rough, blistered paint.

slatted folding tables spruced up with a lick of white latex each season. There are streamlined, contemporary folding chairs and loungers with light-weight aluminum frames and tough synthetic covers. Outdoor furniture can be very basic: a plain white cloth on a practical folding painter's table becomes stylish with a couple of jars of cut flowers and some white candles.

A white wooden slatted folding chair with arms has a beach look; it can be made more comfortable by adding cushions, in blue-and-white ticking, for example.

This sun lounger is made of aluminum with an all-weather fabric cover. Ideal for camping or for stretching out on a deck, beside a pool, or in the backyard.

A vibrant lime green checked cotton deck chair cover is an alternative to traditional stripes.

Accessories

Setting up your outside space is no different from furnishing a room inside. The furniture will largely determine the look, so first decide whether to buy stylish pieces that need to be stored inside during winter or to look around in thrift stores for old metal or wooden tables, benches, and chairs that can be left outside to weather and provide exterior detail all year-round. A simple solution for outside eating is to buy a hardboard tabletop with separate trestles and folding chairs, which can be dressed up with natural fabrics like cotton, muslin, canvas, and ticking. There is enormous scope for creating stylish outside table settings. Forget the days when we were expected to set dinner tables with immaculate sets of flatware and cut-glass crystal. At the most basic level, unbreakable plastic cups, bowls, and plates are useful for children and picnics, while simple white cafeteria china and enameled tin bowls and pitchers creates a plain look that can be embellished with colorful flowers, glowing candles, and bright checked napkins. I have a passion for old glassware and love to mix odd glasses found in flea markets and thrift stores. Whatever items you choose, the only rule is to try to create informal settings that look wonderful yet are simply achieved.

Lighting

Without doubt, the most sensuous outdoor lighting is candlelight at an alfresco supper or the flickering flames of a campfire. The only really pretty electric lights are strings of white lights of the sort used on Christmas trees, which look magical strung in rows across a yard or patio. Cream candles are my favorite lights for outside, and I have a store of empty jars that make really cheap but attractive containers. I also like to use glass hurricane lamps and find that a line of three or four on the table creates pools of soft light. Basic metal lanterns for candles, available at hardware stores, are practical because they can be hung on hooks on the wall. For simple and cheap outdoor lighting, buy bags of votive candles in metal holders. They look great in flickering groups of two dozen or so in the center of a table or placed individually in niches in old brick walls or in lines along windowsills. Votives can burn in a soft breeze but on windy evenings I put them in jars or old flowerpots.

Utensils

A tough white plastic salad bowl is practical for use in the backyard and kitchen and lightweight enough to take on picnics.

A plain wooden tray is ideal for carrying food, drinks, and utensils out to the yard. This one has been given a colorful facelift with blue latex paint.

Dome-shaped food nets conjure up images of old-fashioned country dairies and are efficient at keeping bugs off meat and cheese.

I use simple, basic, functional equipment and utensils for outdoor eating. Invaluable favorites include tough, unbreakable plastic bowls, plates, and mugs, which come in lots of cheerful colors and can be bought cheaply from hardware and chain stores. Tough glassware is not only practical, but looks stylish and is also widely available. For picnics and eating on

If outdoor meals involve children, delicate cups and glasses are likely to end up in smithereens. Play safe with plastic mugs and sturdy glassware that comes in lots of chic shapes and even bounces when dropped.

Reminiscent of those used in school cafeterias, this simple glass water pitcher looks good on an outside table and is cheap and easy to find in hardware stores.

A basic plastic food-storage container, which can be slipped into a bag or knapsack quite conveniently, is always useful for picnics or for carrying sandwiches to school or work.

Enameled tin plates and mugs are great camping basics and also look good at the table. You can find this utilitarian tableware in hardware or camping stores.

Chain stores are good sources of cheap and cheerful, brightly colored plastic tableware, such as these vibrant orange examples that are ideal for picnics and informal outside meals at home.

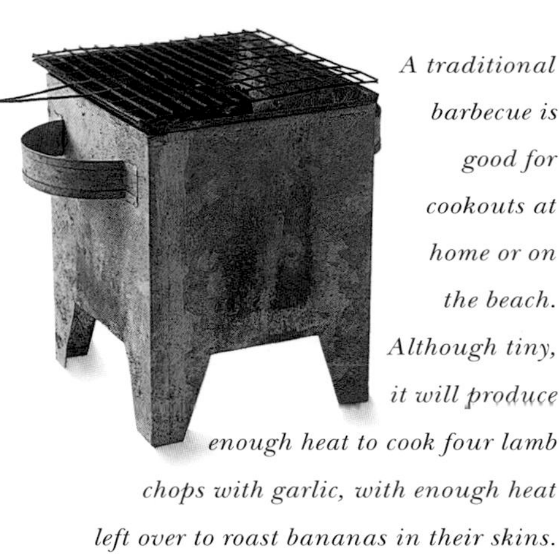

A traditional barbecue is good for cookouts at home or on the beach. Although tiny, it will produce enough heat to cook four lamb chops with garlic, with enough heat left over to roast bananas in their skins.

Napkins and placemats in bright solid colors or checks look best against plain cloths or bare wooden tabletops, and are cheerful even on the cloudiest summer day.

Keep bottles cool with an insulated bottle cooler. This metal one is useful for small bottles or for butter and other fast-melting food.

the move, I am very fond of my tiny metal barbecue, which gives out enough heat to cook a veritable feast of sausages or delicious fresh fish, vegetables, and even bananas and marshmallows. Brewing up cups of steaming coffee on a butane stove with a camping kettle is also a great way of keeping warm when picnicking on a sharp and clear winter day.

A simple galvanized metal pitcher gives a robust, utilitarian look to outdoor tables and is ideal for serving glasses of ice-cold water, or for holding a bunch of freshly cut flowers.

For a truly luxurious picnic, take bottles of drinking water to brew reviving cups of fresh coffee and tea using an old-fashioned camping kettle heated over an open fire or gas camping stove.

Plain white china is the best neutral backdrop for food and the perfect choice for stylish yet simple table settings.

PUTTING IT ALL TOGETH

ER

Create a simple, colorful, textural outdoor retreat where you can unwind on a heap of soft pillows or soak up the heady scent of a climbing rose. Get in touch with the elements by planting a vegetable patch to grow your own nourishing produce. Bring the dining room outdoors for delicious, informal meals, or stretch out on a blanket on the grass for a picnic.

Outside retreats

Many of us, especially urban dwellers, are hemmed in much of the working day and hardly experience fresh air, let alone the sensations of a crisp and frosty morning or the brilliance of a red sunset. Deprived of natural sensations and smells, we humans get depressed, lethargic, and irritable. It is no wonder our sense of well-being increases dramatically when we go outside. Whether it is a terrace, patio, vegetable patch, or a windowsill with a brimming windowbox, having a little bit of outside space to tend to and enjoy creates a diversion from the irritants of daily life—bills, unwanted phone calls, dirty dishes, and so on. Making a room outside—somewhere to eat, drink, sit, contemplate, garden, or play—is no different from decorating and furnishing spaces inside our homes. Outside as well as in, it is important to decide what sort of overall look and feel you wish to create and then be resourceful with your space. The crucial design aspects still apply, such as what color to paint walls, what kind of flooring and fabric to choose, and what sort of furniture will work. It is also about creating a little bit of magic to give you a wonderful retreat in which to sit with a book on warm summer evenings or eat croissants and drink steaming coffee in the crisp morning air.

opposite and right
An elegant, shady Long Island porch is painted white and blue and furnished simply with old wicker tables and chairs with soft feather pillows covered in faded blue-and-white striped ticking.
below left and right
Porch style in the barn-red cabins of the Catskill Mountains makes the most of a selection of simple junk furniture.

Verandas and porches

I grew up believing that only television characters whiled away warm velvet-dark evenings in rocking chairs on wooden porches, listening to crickets. When I finally visited America, I saw that it really happens. I am envious that the climate has made this simple and practical architectural feature a necessity, as well as being a means of enjoying the outdoors in comfort. Among the neat picket fences and lawns of New England, I saw the most charming porches and verandas with pristine white-painted rails and floors. Often enclosed with screens to keep out insects, porches are shady retreats where visitors are entertained and refreshed with pitchers of iced tea. The most stylish and simple porch furniture are informal old wicker chairs and tables, traditional rocking chairs, and hammocks, with pillows in faded blue-and-white striped fabric. Some of the best-looking furniture has been bought for just a few dollars from thrift stores. In the absence of the real thing, the porch look is easy and inexpensive to achieve using stylish old furniture revamped with paint in funky colors and pillows and chair covers in natural fabrics.

above and right *Enclosed with dark green painted metal rails, this London roof terrace is a welcome sun deck, ideal for growing crops of tomatoes and pots of herbs. The look is simple and utilitarian, featuring basic garden tools, old chairs, and a table with a green-and-white checked plastic cloth.*

opposite *A blue-and-white checked blanket and some pillows make a white metal bench a more comfortable resting place.*

Rooftop space

It was not until the rails were installed around the flat roof in the backyard of my London house that I felt it was really an outside room. Before, there was always that niggling feeling that someone might topple over, and, of course, it was out of bounds for children. Apart from installing an outside faucet for watering, which in summer is essential twice a day, the other important task was to lay the pine deck. With a shady courtyard below, the roof is a welcome sun deck, and for that reason I have not bothered with awnings—on hot days we cover up with wide-brimmed hats and sunglasses. To make it more sheltered and secluded, clematis, growing in pots, trails around the rails and over a simple trellis painted with pale mint green latex. Mixing vegetables and flowers makes gardening a more productive and resourceful occupation, and I like to grow vibrant nasturtiums alongside tomatoes and herbs. Even though the garden is only about 35 square feet, there is a sense of space and freedom up among the urban rooftops, and there is nothing better than stealing up there to have a bagel and a cup of coffee on a warm summer morning.

74
73

Beach-hut style

Nearly every seaside town around Britain has a stretch of beach or seafront devoted to higgledy-piggledy strings of small wooden huts that allow you to live, albeit temporarily, in basic fashion without water or electricity beside the ocean. Old-fashioned resort towns like Swanage, Worthing, Whistable, and Bognor have great beach huts—the best ones are in more isolated spots away from town centers. Colors vary from place to place: jaunty blue and white; dark brown creosote; glorious ice cream shades of pistachio, raspberry, and peach; and plain white are all vernacular beach hut paint schemes that will inspire you to create the maritime look at home. Collect pebbles from the beach to make simple still lifes and, for greenery and texture, grow plants like sea kale, which thrive on pebbly beaches. My grandmother rented a beach hut in Devon for wonderful informal picnics with scratchy sand on the floor and fishing nets in the corner. Beach hut gear was appropriately simple: nautical blue-and-white striped canvas deck chairs; a folding table; plain cotton cloths; functional picnic gear in a wicker basket; a camping stove to brew hot drinks; and a warm blanket for naps.

opposite *Traditional beach huts, like these at Worthing, give good ideas for painting a shed or furnishing a deck.* **above, left to right** *Sea kale growing among pebbles is great for creating texture; paint the walls white and rig up a decorative awning in nautical blue-and-white canvas; a white slatted folding chair is practical and stylish seating.*

Continental patio

During the long, hot Andalusian summer, our outside activities take place on the white patio surrounding our house. Rather than opting for rustic limewash, which needs a new coat every spring, we chose basic flat white exterior paint for the walls. The large terra-cotta tiles underfoot were bought from the local dealer at a very low cost. Furniture is basic and portable, so chairs and tables can be moved according to the time of day. I go to Seville to buy traditional Spanish country chairs and stools with rush seats that have a timeless appeal. In contrast to the predominately white background, I like to add splashes of bright color with shocking pink napkins and a bright 1940s green-and-turquoise seersucker tablecloth. Shade is vital, and I designed basic canvas awnings, punched with eyelets and strung to hooks with tough nylon rope.

right *The shady terrace, where the predominance of white is offset by splashes of colorful table linen, is a cool evening retreat.*
opposite *An awning in blue-and-white striped canvas creates shade on the sun-baked patio.*

Urban patio

A plain, simple, utilitarian approach is the key to creating a stylish summer oasis in the confines of a small urban backyard. Rather than being plastered over or repointed, the rough, uneven brick walls have been left to impart their warm, earthy character, together with the worn, mossy red bricks that lie underfoot. This natural, neutral backdrop makes cream canvas chair covers an understandable choice, while a simple white cotton cloth dresses up a folding, rather battered card table. An old wooden meat chest, a mesh food net, a metal flower bucket, and tin lanterns hung on the walls are practical, and add hard-edged yet decorative detail. An old metal shoe rack makes an impromptu tool shed, with

neat shelves for storing bulbs, pots, and tools. An understated glass pitcher, plain bowls, and robust glasses are ideal for the uncluttered look. Greenery is sparse apart from clematis and some rampant buddleia, so anything other than the small topiary boxwood and an amaryllis in a roughly molded terra-cotta pot would be unnecessary.

opposite, left, and above
Utilitarian objects like an old wooden meat chest and a metal shoe rack are useful for storing gardening items in the confines of an urban backyard.

above, below, and right *Blue-and-white checked table linen, white folding chairs, a vase of pink stocks, and a sea green door add cheerful and contemporary coloring to a shady London courtyard.*
opposite *Instant greenery is provided by a young tomato plant in a terra-cotta pot and a tall, architectural-looking bay standard in a metal bucket.*

Colorful courtyard

A simple way to relieve the drabness of a shady courtyard is to use colorful paint and fabric. I transformed a door with eggshell paint in greenish blue, a color that is modern, yet fresh and natural. It looked so good that a wall, rebuilt and pointed with ugly cement, was the next contender for the same color, but in a durable flat latex. Ugly water tanks, fences, and furniture can also be camouflaged with paint—white is always a good color to lift a dull, flat environment. Blue-and-white checked cotton is unfailingly cheerful and chic, and I used a favorite from my stash of colorful cloths. In a space devoid of many plants, buy colorful flowers like bachelor's buttons, stocks, or tulips for informal decorations that can be enjoyed for several days.

opposite and right *Four gnarled grapevines spread a leafy canopy across the terrace of an Andalusian farmhouse. Bright oranges and pinks for tablecloth, napkins, and a throw are a perfect match for stong southern sunlight.*

Vine-covered terrace

A trailing grapevine is a romantic and natural way of shading a terrace. At an ancient Andalusian farmhouse high up among the chestnut and olive groves, four vines, including a knotted and gnarled 20-year-old specimen, have been trained to grow up chestnut posts at 6-foot intervals and across a basic framework of supporting sticks. During the long, hot summers everyone eats lunch and dinner under the vine canopy, which sags with bunches of fat, juicy grapes. In early spring when the vines are not in full leaf, the open spaces are filled in with green fabric awning. Locals say that it takes about three years of careful tending and cutting back to make a fully covered vine canopy. Although a vine outside in a colder climate is unlikely to produce such prodigious fruit, it is possible in a sunny, sheltered, south-facing garden to grow impressive leafy examples. Some garden specialists even import, at vast expense, 50-year-old vines from the south of France. For outside living, an assortment of seats, such as old country benches and chairs, together with new metal garden chairs from a department store, creates a relaxed look. When there are guests to feed, more tables can be brought out under the leafy awning.

this page and opposite
Ideas for understated, natural-looking window-ledge gardens: lavender in a painted vegetable crate (bottom); painted plastic windowboxes planted with ornamental cabbages (below); blue-painted pots of geraniums (right), and a cedar box with aromatic rosemary (opposite).

Windowbox garden

Close to my London home, tubs and pots teeter along the window ledges of highrise buildings, creating brilliant splashes of color. These miniature gardens yielding herbs and vegetables or gaudy favorites like geraniums and marigolds are a vibrant sight in an otherwise grim, gray urban environment. Instead of standard containers, be inventive and revamp an old crate with dark green paint and plant textural lavender. Plastic windowboxes look functional, but they can also be transformed with flat-finish paint in soft mint green or powder blue. Do not stick to the same old planting material either: a dwarf hedge of rosemary, white hyacinths, nasturtiums, or cherry tomatoes are just some ideas.

Vegetable and flower plot

There is something so satisfying about tending a garden that yields flowers for color alongside vegetables to eat. This decorative but utilitarian rectangular plot is bordered by a handmade stick fence and yields a combination of floral and edible produce, including clematis, morning glory, sunflowers, lettuces, cabbages, chard, and beets. In summer, in the cool of early morning or evening, it is a glorious refuge for watering and weeding, soaking up the scents of herbs, and enjoying the fresh, bright colors of the young plants.

above *Simple wooden furniture, like a rustic Adirondack chair (left) and a battered kitchen chair with flaking paint (right), are suitably decorative and functional in a working garden.*

opposite *A mixture of colorful flowers and vegetables grow together in this little enclosed garden in the Catskill Mountains—a truly peaceful oasis in which to sit and contemplate.*

Planting ideas

All gardeners have their own ideas about the key elements in planting a successful space. I view simplicity of layout, together with texture, color, shape, scent, and the edibility of flowers and plants as the most important considerations. I like a sense of order and have a passion for regimented vegetable patches, which have an appeal similar to that of neatly arranged interior rooms. I also like the use of commonplace plants, rather than fancy, exotic varieties that I am happy to leave to real garden experts. Some of my favorites are traditional cottage-garden flowers like roses, dahlias, and clematis, as well as all vegetables—especially cabbages, which look so leafy and decorative. The use of containers, from earthy terra-cotta flowerpots to galvanized metal florist's buckets, is important when space is limited in small yards and on terraces and balconies. Choosing the right size pot, painting it a particular color, and setting it somewhere appropriate are all important. Planting to create texture and color with climbing plants or to make a dramatic statement with tall plants, such as sunflowers or topiary trees like boxwood and bay, are also elements that I consider vitally important to creating a living, visually appealing space.

clockwise from near right *Hollyhocks look distinctive against plain white walls; a low white picket fence is bordered by loosestripe for colorful height and detail; sunflowers grow fast and are ideal for creating tall borders; traditionally used for height in herbaceous borders, delphiniums look good in any setting, such as an urban rooftop.*
opposite *Leeks that have been left to bolt make a dramatic and decorative architectural statement.*

Creating height

Tall, leggy plants provide drama, height, and camouflage. My favorites are sunflowers, which are fun to grow from seed—some reach 10 feet or more, with flowers the size of large plates. Another passion, in pots along a wall, are foxgloves, which shoot up with ease to 4 or 5 feet and have pretty white, purple, or pink bell-shaped flowers that bees love. Delphiniums are easy to grow and also have colorful spiky blooms. Other tall plants that are easy to grow include hollyhocks, which have a timeless appeal and look especially pretty flanking a doorway.

A sense of order

There is something pleasing about small-scale plots with neat rows of vegetables and herbs, tidy flowerbeds with an array of foliage and blooms in colors that blend together or contrast dramatically, and well-raked weeded soil. It proves that humans can contain nature if they methodically dig, plant, and clear. Create natural order in a decorative yet functional garden, with devices such as paths—wide enough for a wheelbarrow—made of wood chippings and bordered with lacy flat-leafed parsley, and rows of wonderful old glass bell jars to nurture seedlings. Enclose the area with a commonplace yet stylish wire fence over which climbers like honeysuckle and trailing tomatoes can be entwined.

top left and right, and opposite *Meticulous well-ordered planting enhances a small ornamental and practical vegetable and flower garden.*
above *A makeshift cold frame constructed from salvaged windows is planted with herbs and salad ingredients.*

Potting ideas

A terra-cotta pot is hard to beat as a container for everything from bulbs to shrubs and herbs. The earthiest pots are the old, roughly molded, hand-thrown ones that are more textural than machine-produced models. Interesting containers are not difficult to find. Raid your local hardware store for galvanized metal buckets, which look great with topiary standards of boxwood, bay, or rosemary, but drill holes for drainage. Bear in mind that the simplest arrangements of only two or three pots can be the most effective. Galvanized troughs look modern and functional on windowsills planted with pretty flowers like hyacinths, narcissi, ornamental cabbages, or herbs.

this page *Almost anything with an earthy, organic look will do as a container for plants, from galvanized metal troughs (below) or an old sink for plants or a makeshift pond (top left) to traditional terra-cotta flowerpots (above).*
opposite *Metal buckets from a hardware store look effective in small groups.*

opposite, clockwise from far left *Plumbago climbing up fine wire; a moss rose trained with string; climbing scarlet beans; nasturtiums growing up a tent of sticks.*
left *Clematis and other climbers trail over chicken wire, creating a leafy paradise for hens.*
below *Stick fencing supports trailing tomatoes.*

Climbers

Train climbing plants with wire and garden string along walls, fences, and trellises, and up pergolas, arbors, and tent-shaped structures. As well as creating color and greenery in a skyward direction, climbers are useful for camouflaging unattractive surfaces. I grow clematis in pots, which runs rampant over the rails around my roof garden and trails up a trellis over a section of harsh red brick wall. The plants soften the hard urban landscape, existing very well in terra-cotta pots if fed regularly with manure and watered copiously. Other favorite climbers include plumbago, which has beautiful starlike flowers; climbing roses like *Rosa* 'Madame Alfred Carrière' and *R.* 'New Dawn'; grapevines, which are perfect for making shady arbors; jasmine, especially varieties that produce the most wonderful heady scent at night; and passionflowers—I love the purplish blooms and orange fruits. Climbers are also handy if space is short. In a vegetable plot, for example, nasturtiums, tomatoes, beans, cucumbers, and zucchini can all be trained up stakes and along fences.

Flowers and vegetables

For economic reasons, traditional cottage gardens always contained a mixture of flowers for cutting and vegetables for consumption by the family. Many gardeners, who are not necessarily interested in self-sufficiency, adopt the same approach for purely decorative reasons, since many vegetables and herbs hold ornamental appeal. Others, who enjoy eating the fruits of their labors, delight in growing a combination of the decorative and the edible, with everything from beans and potatoes to roses and sweet peas jostling for position in one patch. I look forward to late summer, when tiny plots are ablaze with color in the form of big, floppy green cabbages and lettuces, contrasted with the gaudy, pinks, yellows, and oranges of dahlias. For dramatic contrast, plant round-headed lettuces next to tall, gangly alliums with their pompom flowers. A combination of chives, mint and parsley, can be used to create pretty, textural edgings, while tall climbing plants like beans, tomatoes, and cucumbers make attractive green perimeters. Layers of straw mulch, which is used for keeping the soil warm, also looks decorative.

opposite *Floppy green cabbages planted with a colorful array of dahlias in a working garden in London are good examples of combined floral and edible produce.*

left and above

This ornamental flower and vegetable patch in the Catskill Mountains measures just 20 x 30 feet. It is bisected with hard, dirt paths and planted with neat rows of lettuces, chard, and cabbages, interspersed with colorful blooms such as daisies and vibrant marigolds.

right *An apple tree from an espaliered row encloses a simple vegetable and herb garden.*

opposite, clockwise from top left *A tent-shaped wire topiary frame for climbing plants like ivy, nasturtiums, vine tomatoes, or beans; as the plant grows, the stems can be trained around the wire and tied in place with string. An aromatic rosemary standard is trimmed into an architectural shape; the clippings can be dried for use in cooking. A squat boxwood ball looks good on its own or arranged with others along a balcony or terrace.*

Clipped and trained

When we think of topiary, it is usually yew hedges clipped into the amusing shapes of dogs, cats, chickens, or other favored animals. On a smaller scale—available from good garden centers—there are evergreen shrubs like boxwood and bay clipped into squat balls or taller, leggy stems with pompom tops. These all look good in small paved areas and require little maintenance apart from watering and regular trimming with shears to keep them in shape. There are topiary wire frames in tent and ball shapes that are good for training things like nasturtiums, vine tomatoes, and beans. In the walled gardens of old country houses, you often see the espaliered branches of exotic pear and apple varieties that have been trained to grow flat and spread out in fan shapes. An espalier framework is made with a series of upright posts supporting several wires strained horizontally to secure the branches. An espalier-trained tree is restricted to pairs of branches that stretch out horizontally from the trunk and are secured to the espalier for support. Espaliered trees also make an unusual natural fence or partition in a small yard.

Eating

Eating and drinking are sensual pleasures, and become more so if the ingredients are delicious and the surroundings heavenly. Simplicity is the key to making the most of dining outdoors on a balmy evening or a sunny afternoon. Invest in good, basic cooking tools, such as sharp knives, solid mixing bowls, and pans with heavy bottoms. Keep tableware simple with plain white china and durable but good-looking glassware. Use white sheets for everyday tablecloths, but for special occasions put out beautiful crisp linen. Buy the best cheese, fish, meat, fruit, vegetables, and wine that you can afford, and prepare meals that involve minimal preparation. Serve plenty of healthy salads and raw vegetables and enjoy experimenting with the addition of homegrown herbs. Set the table in a sheltered, shady environment and keep furniture basic and portable: a trestle table and folding director's chairs are ideal. At night light candles in lanterns, jars, or glass holders, and decorate the table with pitchers of freshly cut herbs or flowers, such as roses or marigolds. Keep picnic equipment to a minimum, with a cooler and blanket. Set up under a tree or in a sheltered sand dune and build a campfire to cook sausages or pack plenty of sandwiches, and good chocolate and fruit.

opposite **opposite** *A picnic by the ocean on the deck of a beach hut is simple and stylish with a white folding chair, blue-and-white napkins, and a practical big straw basket.*
clockwise from right *Cucumber chunks; eggs frying on a campfire; and bread with fresh crab.*

Picnics

My family are enthusiastic picnickers who relish the freedom of eating informally outside at any time of year. We head off to one of the parks in London, or, when we need to blow away the cobwebs, we go farther afield to a safe, sandy beach, such as Camber Sands in Sussex or Studland Bay in Dorset. The best picnics are simple and uncomplicated affairs. For meals by the ocean, I pack a basket with blue-and-white striped napkins, a box of matches, and a bottle cooler. In a sheltered spot by a breakwater or in a sand dune, we make a campfire with driftwood and dried seaweed or light a little metal barbecue for a cookout after a dip in the ocean. Fried eggs or sausages are wedged between chunks of good chewy bread. Sometimes we buy a local dressed crab, which, seasoned with lemon and pepper, we spread onto wholewheat bread. On cold but bright winter days, I pack a warm wool plaid blanket, bars of good chocolate, a thermos of potato and leek soup, and a box of bagels with lox and cream cheese. Other picnic goodies include wedges of delicious cheese with oat crackers and cheese straws, chunks of tomatoes dipped in a little salt, a jar of olives, large chunks of cucumber, and crisp apples.

above and opposite *Simple food suits the pared-down look of an outdoor table with white cloth and tableware, mesh food nets, candles in glass holders, and a few stems of tuberose, which smell heavenly at night.*
right *Roasted peppers and eggplant; roasted diced potatoes; tomatoes with olive oil and basil.*

Simple supper

I have a passion for vegetables, especially roasted, and find them one of the simplest, tastiest accompaniments to grilled or barbecued fish and meat. For summer suppers, I chop up potatoes, complete with skin, eggplant, red peppers, onions, and zucchini, and place them in a flat roasting pan with a good douse of olive oil and lemon juice, some garlic, rosemary, or basil,

and cook them in the middle of a hot oven, turning regularly, for about 45 minutes or until everything is soft and nicely browned. Any leafy green vegetable, such as cabbage, is delicious steamed, then cooked for a minute or so in butter and mint. Staples like baked potatoes, impaled on a skewer for faster cooking, are another favorite served with butter, salt, and pepper. Salads of lettuce, rocket, or other seasonal leaves are essential, as are homegrown tomatoes, often chopped with basil, garlic, salt, olive oil, and lemon juice. In keeping with my pared-down approach to cooking, I cover the table with a crisp white cloth and serve food in large white enameled metal casseroles, which look stylish alongside simple, plain white dishes.

Lunch break

When I am dashing around for work, grabbing sandwiches to eat on the run, I think wistfully of my Spanish friends who sit down daily to a relaxing and civilized lunch, either at home where they tuck into something like a tortilla or in a bar that serves delicious tapas of squid or fried fish. Things are happily different on vacation, when there is time to sit down to eat and talk in the middle of the day. Pasta is the top request in my household and, as long as there is a good bed of steaming al dente spaghetti to mix the sauce in, I can get away with serving ingredients that are otherwise unacceptable to the youngest members, such as strong cheese, herbs, and—worst of all—lots of garlic. Tomato sauce, made with tasty homegrown tomatoes, is one of the easiest and most delicious things to serve with pasta. Simply sauté three or four large, peeled, chopped tomatoes in olive oil and garlic until they are half cooked. Seasoned with parsley or basil, this highly aromatic, slightly crunchy, tomato sauce is best with a long pasta like tagliatelle or spaghetti. As soon as pumpkins are available in late summer, I cook a couple of pounds of the chopped flesh in salted water until soft. After draining, I sauté it in olive oil and garlic for a few minutes, and then add ¼ cup of light cream, ⅓ cup of grated Parmesan, and some nutmeg or basil to bring out the flavor of the pumpkin. Then, if I can be bothered, I pulverize the mixture in a blender. When heated up, this utterly delicious pale-orange sauce can be served with any kind of pasta. Fresh mushrooms cooked in butter, garlic, and parsley are another delicious accompaniment for pasta. Lasagne is also a top-ten favorite, and, instead of ground beef, I sometimes use cooked zucchini, eggplant, and tomatoes in between layers of béchamel sauce, pasta sheets, and grated Parmesan.

above, left, and opposite *Make simple lunchtime pasta treats sauced with chopped homegrown tomatoes and herbs; serve with a wedge of fresh bread and a glass of cold white wine.*

Birthday party

It is wishful thinking to imagine that junk foods, such as chips, candy, and colas, are not expected at a children's party. When my daughter requested pizza for her sixth birthday party, I felt mean when I refused her the bought kind that oozes preservatives, which she had set her sights on. So I was faced with the challenge of producing healthy pizza that would please a disgruntled birthday girl. Using thick slices of crusty bread, I toasted them on one side. Then I rubbed the uncooked side with garlic, trickled on olive oil, and added cooked chopped tomatoes. I topped the slices with grated parmesan and placed them under the broiler until bubbling—a great success. I gave in and bought bottles of the least violently colored sodas, but offered pitchers of ice-cold water, which were just as popular. I also served slices of orange and watermelon, cold from the fridge. We made an outrageously rich chocolate cake, which was decorated with blackberries and candles. Rather than using drab paper plates and cups, I bought brightly colored plastic plates, cups, and straws from a local discount store, and set the table with a length of bright blue plastic cloth.

opposite, left, and above
Chocolate cake and home-made pizza are key edibles for a children's birthday party. Plastic, in bright colors for the tablecloth, plates, cups, and straws, is both practical and festive tableware.

above *Delicious cupcakes are decorated with frosting and fresh marigold petals.*
opposite *A vibrant tea-table setting with a contemporary pink and orange color scheme provided by the tablecloth, napkins, and a wool throw. A vase of roses and marigolds adds an extra brilliant touch of color.*

Afternoon tea

A glorious summer afternoon is a wonderful excuse to make something sticky and sweet to eat outside in the shade, under a tree or on the deck, with a cup of steaming and refreshing Earl Grey tea. Make this indulgent treat a special occasion with a jazzy orange tablecloth and a pitcher of bright marigolds, zinnias, or roses. For a traditional English tea, make bite-size cucumber and cream cheese sandwiches. Bake some cupcakes—they really are very simple and quick to make. Mix together 5 tablespoons of sugar, 2 eggs, and 1 cup and 2 tablespoons of self-rising flour, then spoon heaping teaspoons of the mixture into little paper cups or greased muffin pans and bake at 350° for ten minutes. When the cakes are cool, decorate them with frosting and fresh or crystallized flower petals, like pansy, marigold, rose, nasturtium, geranium, lavender, and borage (see page 66). Other teatime goodies include freshly baked biscuits, which can be thrown together in a matter of minutes. Simply mix 1⅔ cups of self-rising flour, 4 tablespoons of butter, 2 tablespoons of sugar, 1 beaten egg, and ⅓ cup of milk in a bowl. Roll out the dough, cut it into rounds, then place them on a greased baking tray and cook at 450° for ten minutes. Try serving them warm with crème fraîche and homemade blackberry jelly. Oat bars, made with corn syrup, butter, and rolled oats, are deliciously chewy, and another favorite are slabs of crumbly shortbread, especially good fresh from the oven.

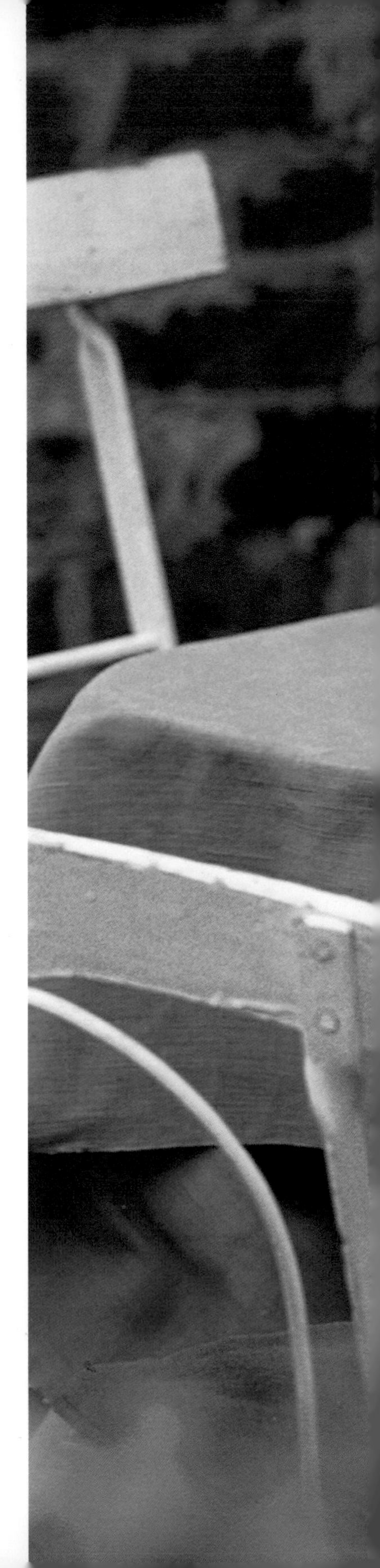

left *Pale blue-and-white stripes combined with minty green is a stylish and understated color scheme that is perfect for eating out on a wooden veranda. The folding director's chairs are covered in tough canvas and can be stored easily at the end of summer. Simple metal hurricane lanterns, and pitchers of blue scabious and bachelor's buttons complete the tidy, relaxed effect.*

opposite *Ideas for tasty summer desserts include raspberry mold in chunky 1930s-style glasses that were picked up cheaply from a thrift store, and a plum pie, which is delicious served with a scoop of crème fraîche.*

Summer desserts

With so many fruits in season—cherries, strawberries, and raspberries — making desserts for summer meals has endless possibilities and can be really simple. My favorite fruit whip, made with thick cream or low-fat fromage blanc, is good old-fashioned strawberry, which I serve with short-bread cookies; other successful whips include lemon, quince, and blackberry.

Pies are always a good idea, and, made with plums, peaches, or apples in a rich, buttery pie crust, are delicious hot or cold. Fruit molds made with gelatin and fresh raspberry, straw-berry, grape, or peach juice, look really pretty in individual glasses. There is also traditional English summer pud-ding, perfect for when all the berry fruits are in season, like red and black currants, raspberries, and blueberries.

Breakfast

Good coffee, fresh bread, butter, and homemade jelly are my essentials for a civilized breakfast. I like to make strong Italian espresso coffee in an old-fashioned percolator, and unless the bread is still warm from the baker, I prefer it heated up in the oven or toasted. There are so many fancy breads to choose from nowadays, but toasted hunks from a healthy whole-wheat loaf or a crusty white loaf are as tasty as they are filling. Breakfast is a chance to indulge in eating natural honey and homemade jellies and marmalades. When bitter Seville oranges are in season in January, I always promise myself I will make a batch of marmalade, which, interestingly, the Spanish themselves do not eat—it seems to be a curious British habit. Fresh fruit on the table—figs, watermelon, peaches, and apples in the summer, and fat juicy oranges in the winter—is always a treat, and an easy alternative source of vitamin C is a large glass of unsweetened orange juice. Unless it is the weekend or a vacation, I like breakfast to be a fairly quick and efficient meal, with basic white plates and mugs set on a practical yet cheery plastic checked cloth.

opposite, above, and right

An alfresco breakfast of fresh fruit, bread, and honey, washed down with a cup of strong black coffee, is a perfect way to start the day. Simple white plates and mugs set on an attractive plastic cloth are also key elements, while shade is provided by home-made canvas awnings.

Mood

It might sound like a cliché, but it invigorates the senses to be outside, in touch with nature and the elements that surround you: water, light, scent, and texture. It is delicious to be outdoors after a heavy rain storm, feeling the cool, damp air and seeing leaves glistening with water or rose petals plastered to the ground like wet confetti. On long, hot, sunny afternoons, any shady spot becomes a welcome retreat, and it is a luxury to lie in dappled light under a tree, eating ice cream or enjoying a lazy picnic. Gardens smell of so many things: fragrant roses and honeysuckle; aromatic herbs like rosemary and lavender, which are very hardy and can be grown just about anywhere; and after a storm, the heady aroma of earthy dampness. Scents are evocative of time and place, and the fragrance of cut grass or a particular rose can take me back to my childhood. When temperatures soar, the mere sound of water—a tinkling fountain or a gushing outdoor shower or faucet—is a relief to a hot and bothered body. Try to find the time to hide away outside in the same way as you might curl up with a good book in a comfortable chair by the fire. Take breakfast outside on a warm summer morning, or stretch out on a blanket on the grass to catch up on a novel.

Lazy afternoon

Looking back to my childhood, I recall days when we walked to the park and ate ice creams on a blanket under a leafy tree. The row of stores opposite, their striped awnings lowered, took on a sleepy feel. Afternoons were long and languid, and best spent in the dappled cool of the large apple tree in our backyard reading, drinking lemonade, and eating cookies. Squinting at the afternoon sun from my shady retreat under the awning at our house in Spain, time has passed but the feeling is the same. With echoes of those carefree days, it is an unsurpassed luxury to soak up the enveloping warmth and enjoy a long, lazy lunch of salads, fresh bread, and hunks of cheese.

left and opposite

On a long, hot summer afternoon, keep cool in the dappled light of a shady tree and enjoy a lazy, informal lunch, with plenty of healthy salads, fresh bread, and juicy fruit.

right *Tranquility in a rain-soaked backyard, with rose petals plastered to the ground and the greenery enlivened and intensified in color.*
below *Alchemilla bent double with glistening drops of water.*

Rain-soaked garden

Sometimes the summer air becomes stuffy and oppressive. The heat intensifies until you feel the first twinges of a headache; you drink lots of water; clothes feel tight and uncomfortable, and it becomes an effort to attempt the simplest chore. Outside, the air draws closer, and the light assumes a dull, flat quality. In the yard there is a sense of anticipation; nothing stirs, and the plants seem stifled by the lack of breeze. The air is thick with the dry, scorched smells of grass and earth. The storm clouds gather and darken, and when the first droplets of rain splash and scatter the dusty surface, there is a sense of relief. First one drop, then another, and then the sky empties itself like a giant bucket. The thunder rumbles and roars, and lightning snakes through the sky. Heavy rain is wonderfully cleansing and leaves the outdoors sparkling with wetness. It is intoxicating to walk among the dripping plants and drink in the moist, heady, earthy air. Under bare feet the soaking grass feels spongy, cool, and more accommodating. Vegetation is greener, and leaves and petals are shiny like pebbles washed by the tide, while wet paths house light-reflecting puddles. Serious gardeners dread summer rain storms, which seem to arrive when gardens are at their peak. Yet although it may be disastrous for prize blooms, voluptuous flower heads, with drooping petals ready to fall, assume a fragile rain-sodden beauty after being buffeted and bruised by the elements.

Scent

The intoxicating smell of rambling roses, heady jasmine, or the lingering sweetness of cut tuberoses are, like all outdoor smells, evocative of a time and place. From my childhood I particularly remember the golden *Rosa* 'Peace' blooms in our garden, which smelled like delicious soap; the fresh, sweet haylike scent of newly cut grass; and the strange herby smell that lingered on your hands after picking tomatoes. Some of the most aromatic plants are lavender, thyme, chamomile, and rosemary. Lavender is a hardy evergreen that is easy to grow in pots or as a decorative hedge or border edging. The spiky stems with their delicate purple flowers are typical of summer and smell delicious when brushed against. Lavender can be hung in bunches to dry and the flowers used to fill

sachets to scatter among clothes in drawers. Lavender is also useful for adding scent and bulk to potpourri. Hardy thyme and chamomile are pretty, compact plants that are easy to grow between paving stones and emit fresh, herby fragrances when crushed underfoot. A carpet of chamomile on an area of lawn is another delicious way to impart scent. Thyme is a valuable herb for flavoring meat and fish, while chamomile makes a delicious tea. Rosemary is another wonderfully aromatic plant that is easy to grow and looks pretty either as low hedges, in pots, or clipped into topiary standards. I dry stems of rosemary and hang them by the oven for flavoring everything from pasta to chicken. I also use pitchers or vases of fresh rosemary stems to decorate summer tables.

opposite far left
Thyme planted in cracks between paving stones adds soft greenery and a delicious scent when crushed underfoot.

left and opposite
Lavender is aromatic while it is growing, and once dried the flowers can be used to make scented sachets and potpourris.

above *Nestling in the shade of an olive tree, a lightweight folding chair, dressed in a simple cotton pull-on loose cover, makes a peaceful retreat—the perfect place to enjoy a quiet hour or two catching up on your reading.*
right *A shady patch of grass, beneath leafy branches strung with metal candle lanterns, is furnished with a traditional moss-encrusted wooden bench. Next to it, on an old metal table spread with a pink-and-white checked cotton cloth, are bowls of radishes for healthy nibbling.*

Simple retreats

Caught up in the demands of work and home life in an age that demands our immediate reaction to every bleep of a pager or fax transmission, it is important to find time and space to sit, reflect, read a book, or do nothing but soak up the beauty of a warm afternoon or evening. Make your own peaceful retreat with a favorite chair in the most sensuous part of your backyard: by a scented rose, perhaps, or in a spot that gets lots of sun, or in a patch of wild grass and flowers. Set up a table and eat lunch there—a sandwich full of good things like broiled vegetables or crisp lettuce leaves and tasty cheese, with fresh strawberries to follow. My place to hide away from daily demands is my tiny rooftop garden, which is cool and refreshing in the early morning and the perfect place to enjoy breakfast with the newspaper. In the middle of the day I can stretch out on a blanket on the deck and soak up some warm sunshine. At dusk I like to watch the sky turn pink, light some candles, and relish the peace, which is shattered only from time to time as an ambulance or police car shrieks toward another urban drama.

Top *Simple folding chairs in pretty colors are practical for use in the house and outdoors, and they are easy to carry to a favorite patch to sit in comfort among uncut grass and wildflowers.*
bottom left and right *A traditional bench painted basic garden green can be equipped with pillows for extra comfort.*

Water

It is refreshing to cool off in the heat of the day with an invigorating swim or cold shower. In the scorching mid-day sun, even the sound of water is a relief to a hot, sticky body. It makes life so much easier if you can install a faucet outside for watering plants and to fill refreshing bowls of water to splash you down or soak your feet and hands when the heat becomes too intense. Few of us have the available space or funds required for a pool, but an outside shower is a reasonably inexpensive luxury. Freestanding or fixed to a wall or fence, a simple shower head with a deck beneath is the perfect way to make you feel as if you have just had a reviving dip.

above and right *Install an outdoor shower to refresh yourself in the height of summer. For maximum style, choose simple, functional shapes for shower heads and pipes, mount them on a wall or fence tucked away in a secluded corner, and plan a suitable surface for drainage, such as a ceramic shower tray or a hardwood deck.*

opposite *An outdoor faucet, such as this traditional one bought cheaply from a plumbing supplier, makes watering the garden easy and allows you to create an impromptu outside washing area, with an enameled bowl, soft towel, and your favorite soap.*

Shady summer evening

On a balmy evening, move outside to watch the softening light, lengthening shadows, and intensifying hues of a technicolor sunset. As dusk falls, it is a peaceful time to sit and reflect on the day's activities. In keeping with this tranquil mood, make your outdoor room a calm oasis furnished in neutral whites and creams. These colors are my favorites for fabrics and furniture on the patio of our house in Spain, where evenings in summer are spent enjoying the fragrant warm air. The table is laid with candles in metal lanterns and vases of tuberoses, and I bring out cream canvas director's chairs, which are really comfortable for lazing in. We light the barbecue, load it with fish steaks, and make simple salads of tomatoes and green leaves. In the courtyard, the bench seating is covered with assorted soft pillows in plain canvas and blue-and-white stripes—ideal for stretching out on after a hearty supper.

right *Neutral fabrics brighten the terrace as the light fades at dusk.*
opposite *Pillows in white and understated stripes for relaxing in comfort.*

right *Picnic on the grass with a blue and white theme on a sunny late-summer afternoon: a crisp blue-and-white checked cotton cloth and deck chairs covered in cheerful plain and striped cotton.*
opposite *Pack a picnic tea in a traditional metal lunchbox and choose tea-time favorites like oat bars, bagels with jelly, or slabs of fruitcake.*

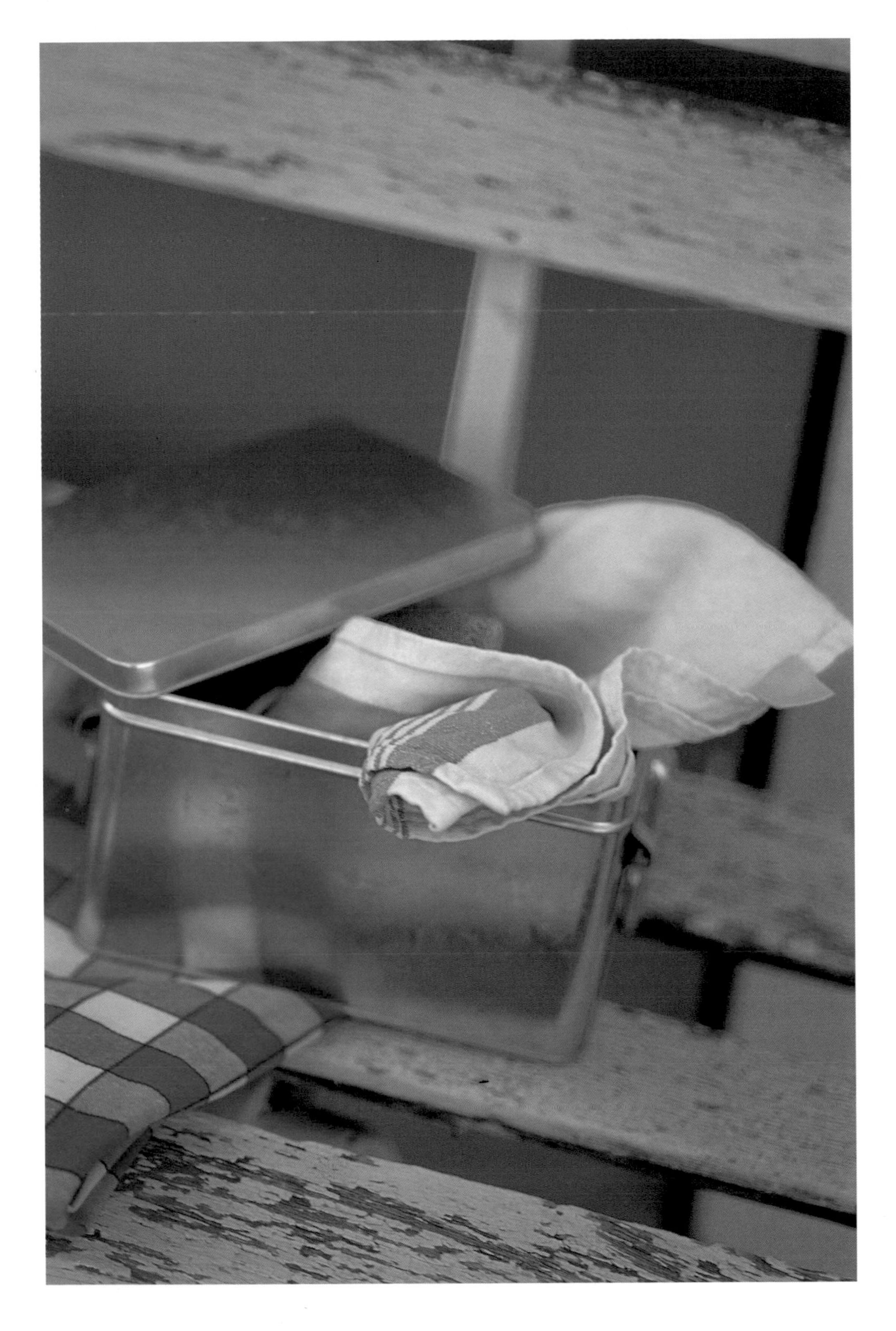

Soft grass

Grass is the perfect outdoor surface for lying on and gazing up at a cloudless summer sky. It comes in many guises: a luxurious stretch of immaculately tended, manicured green lawn; a scorched and bristly field; a lush uncultivated sweep of tall, swaying grasses and poppies; or a clipped and cosseted park. It is good to feel grass between your toes or tickling your hands as you idly pick clover and daisies to make into chains. Then there is the wetness of grass early in the morning, glistening with silvery drops of dew, or the soft dampness of a refeshed lawn after a summer rain storm. Pitching camp on a patch of soft, spongy grass is one of the most relaxing ways to spend a hot weekend afternoon, and a long, languid picnic will invigorate the soul and improve your mood after the stresses of the week. Some of the best picnics are to be had at a local park, where you can always find a welcoming shady tree or a secluded sunny patch. Essentials for picnics on the grass are, in addition to a cooler packed with delicious food and drink, a cloth to lay your food on and a blanket or, if you prefer, some lightweight deck chairs on which to sit.

Credits

Page 7
Ash pergola in the garden of Dean Riddle, Phoenicia, NY.
Page 8
Shed in the garden of Dean Riddle, Phoenicia, NY.
Page 16
Paint swatches from top: Ralph Lauren Whites Collection (WH05A Picket Fence); Ralph Lauren Whites Collection (WH01A Design Studio); Ralph Lauren Whites Collection (WH06B Writers Parchment; Ralph Lauren Safari Collection (SA10D Rice); Jelly glass, After Noah.
Page 17
Wooden picket fence windowbox, Jerry's Home Store.
Page 18
Blue-and-white checked placemat, Crate & Barrel.
Page 19
Paint swatches from top: Martha Stewart (Bluestar); Ralph Lauren Round Hill Collection (RH01C Tropical Colonnade); Ralph Lauren Country Collection (CO03A Southampton Blue); Ralph Lauren Country Collection (CO13A Blue Ridge Mountain).
Page 20
Paint swatches from top: Benjamin Moore Regal Collection (499 Glazed Green); Sanderson (Spectrum 40–04 Sunny Green); Martha Stewart (Basketweave Green); Benjamin Moore Regal Collection (501 Mesquite).
Page 23
Wool rug, Designers Guild; cricket chair, IKEA; tulips, McQueens; paint swatches from top: Ralph Lauren Country Collection (CO18A Veranda Iris); Ralph Lauren Santa Fe Collection (SF07C Fresco); Ralph Lauren Country Collection (CO08C Clover Patch; Martha Stewart (June Iris)
Page 24
Paint swatches from top: Martha Stewart (Cantaloupe); Martha Stewart (Old Brick); Ralph Lauren Santa Fe Collection (SF15A Desert Rose); Ralph Lauren Santa Fe Collection (SF01A Squash Blossom); flowerpots, Smith & Hawken.
Page 25
Scented candles, Price's Patent Candle Co; napkins, Designers Guild; plastic plate and cutlery, Woolworth's; pumpkins, Wayside Organics.
Page 26
Paint swatches from top: Ralph Lauren Safari Collection (SA12B Nigerian Peony); Martha Stewart (Oat Straw); Ralph Lauren Safari Collection (SF06D Chamois); Martha Stewart (Beeswax); napkin and placemat, Crate & Barrel.
Page 27
Yellow bowl, El Corte Ingles.
Pages 28–9
House of Ellen O'Neill, Long Island, NY.
Page 36
Stick border (bottom left) and stick fence (bottom right) in the garden of Dean Riddle, Phoenicia, NY.
Page 37
Garden of Timothy Leese and Robert Chance, Norfolk, England; blue and green PVC, Habitat; deck chair in checked cotton fabric by Designers Guild; gate in the garden of Nancy McCabe, northwest Connecticut.
Page 38–9
Garden of Nancy McCabe, northwest Connecticut.
Page 40
Shed in the community garden of John Matheson, London.
Page 42–3
Planting by Nancy McCabe in her garden in northwest Connecticut.
Page 44
Fence painted in Prion outdoor paint by Crown-Berger in the garden of Vanessa de Lisle, fashion consultant, London.
Page 45
Trellis (top left) painted in Prion outdoor paint by Crown-Berger; twiggy supports (far right, top and center) in the garden of Nancy McCabe, northwest Connecticut; stick fence (bottom right) in the garden of Dean Riddle, Phoenicia, NY.
Page 46
Clockwise from top left: old shears, Avant Garden; trowel, dibble and fork, Clifton Nurseries; besom broom, Avant Garden; basket, Clifton Nurseries; plastic apron and gardening gloves, Homebase.
Page 47
Clockwise from top left: plastic trash bag, Homebase; tote, Homebase; Andalusian pitchfork and old shovel, Avant Garden; rubber boots with leather lining, Avant Garden; wooden plant labels, The Conran Shop; raffia and string, Homebase.
Page 48–9
Metal plant trough, The Conran Shop.
Page 50
Weathered terra-cotta flowerpots, General Trading Company.
Page 51
Clockwise from center: low planter, Avant Garden; rhubarb forcer, Avant Garden; tall flowerpot, Avant Garden; old flowerpot with amaryllis, The Conran Shop; hanging pot, Clifton Nurseries, with a wash of white and terra-cotta latex paint by Cole & Son.
Page 52
Clockwise from top left: metal planter, The Conran Shop; metal lunchbox, Muji; metal bucket, IKEA; metal bucket with lavender, Paula Pryke Flowers; metal bucket, G J Chapman.
Page 54
Green and blue plastic flowerpots, The Conran Shop.
Page 55
Wooden picket fence windowbox, Jerry's Home Store; plastic windowbox, Clifton Nurseries, painted in powder blue latex paint by Farrow & Ball; ornamental cabbages, McQueens; seed tray, The Conran Shop.
Page 72
Bench painted in color 819 by Benjamin Moore & Co.
Page 74–5
1 ribbed cotton, The Conran Shop; 2 cotton, Sanderson; 3 linen, Sanderson; PVC-coated cotton, John Lewis; 5 checked sheer cotton, Habitat; 6 washed, cotton, The Conran Shop; 7 plain dye canvas cotton, John Lewis; 8 cotton duck, Whaleys Ltd; 9 cotton, Habitat; 10 cotton, Designers Guild; 11 ribbed cotton, The Conran Shop; 12 silk, Designers Guild; 13 ribbed cotton, stylist's own; 14 ribbed cotton, The Conran Shop; 15 cotton ticking, Ian Mankin; 16 cotton, Ian Mankin; 17 striped cotton, Laura Ashley; 18 checked cotton, Ian Mankin; 19 cotton ticking, Ian Mankin; 20 PVC-coated viscose and polyester, John Lewis; 21 solid rib caustic cotton, Habitat; 22 plain cotton, Designers Guild; 23 cotton check, Designers Guild; 24 sheer cotton, Habitat; 25 PVC, Habitat; 26 PVC Habitat; 27 PVC, Habitat.
Page 76
Clockwise from top left: blue wooden bench, IKEA; aluminum-frame rocking chair, Graham & Green; wood folding table painted in white latex paint, Habitat.
Page 77
Clockwise from top left: potting

bench, IKEA, painted in Dulux Definitions (1030 Monsoon), deck chair, Jerry's Home Store; folding table, IKEA; old deck chair in green cotton check, Designers Guild; sun lounger with aluminum frame, Graham & Green.

Pages 78–9
Pitcher, Ruby Beets Antiques.

Page 80
Clockwise from top right: glass storm lamps, Jerry's Home Store; votive candle, IKEA; lantern, B'zar; hurricane lantern, Jerry's Home Store; candles, Price's Patent Candle Co; glass storm lamp, The Dining Room Shop.

Page 82
Clockwise from top left: white plastic bowl, Divertimenti; wooden tray, Habitat, painted in Sanderson Spectrum 23–05 Easter Egg; plastic mug, Debenhams; glass, The Conran Shop; tin plate, Blacks Camping Shop; plastic lunchbox, Divertimenti; water pitcher, Staines Catering Equipment; food net, Divertimenti.

Page 83
Clockwise from top left: plastic plate, knife and fork, Woolworth's; Greek barbecue, Young & D; gingham paper napkins, Paperchase; orange-and-pink checked napkin, Designers Guild; metal pitcher, Jerry's Home Store; white bowl, Staines Catering Equipment; kettle, stylist's own; bottle cooler, Blacks Camping Shop.

Page 86–7
Chairs and cotton covers, The Conran Shop.

Page 88
Blue-and-white striped cotton cushion covers, Ralph Lauren Home Collection; location (top): house of Ellen O'Neill, Long Island, NY; location (bottom left and right): house of Dean Riddle, Phoenicia, NY.

Page 89
House of Ellen O'Neill, Long Island, NY.

Page 90
Metal sieve, After Noah; chair and wooden trellis painted in Sanderson Spectrum 39–03 Salad Green; checked plastic fabric tablecloth, John Lewis; watering can, Tobias and the Angel.

Page 91
Blue checked wool blanket, Melin Tregwynt.

Page 94
Blue-and-green cloth, Tobias and the Angel; pitcher, The Conran Shop; folding chairs, Habitat.

Page 95
Wooden folding table, Habitat.

Page 96
Folding chairs, Habitat, with covers made in cotton duck from Whaleys Ltd; food net, Divertimenti; wooden food chest, After Noah.

Page 97
Metal shoe rack, After Noah.

Page 98
Cloth in blue checked cotton, Designers Guild; white bowl, The Conran Shop.

Page 99
Metal bucket, IKEA; bay tree, Clifton Nurseries.

Page 100–1
Garden of Nick and Hermione Tudor, Finca El Moro, Spain.

Page 102
Plastic windowboxes, Clifton Nurseries, painted in powder blue latex paint by Farrow & Ball.

Page 103
Cedar windowbox, Clifton Nurseries; location: house of David and Carolyn Fuest, London.

Page 104–5
Vegetable and flower plot of Dean Riddle, Phoenicia, NY.

Page 108
Location (bottom right): community garden of John Matheson, London.

Page 109
Blue bench, IKEA.

Page 110
Vegetable and flower garden of Nancy McCabe, northwest Connecticut.

Page 112
Metal buckets, IKEA and G J Chapman; small metal bin, Paula Pryke Flowers.

Page 113
Metal planters, The Conran Shop.

Page 115
Chicken coop in the garden of Nancy McCabe, northwest Connecticut; stick fence in the garden of Dean Riddle, Phoenicia, NY.

Page 117
Vegetable and flower garden of Dean Riddle, Phoenicia, NY.

Page 118
Herb and vegetable garden of Nancy McCabe, northwest Connecticut.

Page 120
Glasses, El Corte Ingles; food net, Divertimenti.

Page 124
Food nets, Ruby Beet Antiques; storm lamps, Habitat; pitcher and bowl, The Conran Shop; metal flower bucket, The Conran Shop.

Page 127
Folding chairs and wooden folding tables painted in white latex paint, Habitat.

Page 128–9
Tablecloth in blue PVC fabric from Habitat; straws, IKEA.

Page 130
Checked blanket and checked napkins, Designers Guild; tablecloth in orange cotton fabric from The Conran Shop.

Page 132
Metal hurricane lanterns, Jerry's Home Store; metal pitcher, Jerry's Home Store; striped cloth and napkins, Jerry's Home Store; folding chairs, Old Town.

Page 133
Dessert glasses, After Noah; tray, Habitat, painted in Sanderson Spectrum 23–05 Easter Egg.

Page 134
White plates, IKEA.

Page 136–7
Garden of Vanessa de Lisle, fashion consultant, London.

Page 138–9
Garden of Lisa Bynon and Mona Nehrenberg, Sag Harbor, NY.

Pages 140–1
Garden of Vanessa de Lisle, fashion consultant, London.

Page 144
Cloth in checked cotton, Designers Guild.

Page 146
Bowl and cotton towel, The Conran Shop.

Page 147
Location (right): garden of Lisa Bynon and Mona Nehrenberg, Sag Harbor, NY.

Page 148
Folding director's chairs, Heal's.

Page 149
White folding table painted in white latex paint, Habitat; cushions in bold striped cotton by Laura Ashley and narrow striped cotton by Ian Mankin.

Page 150
Checked cloth, Divertimenti.

Page 151
Metal lunchbox, Muji.

Page 152–3
Vegetable and flower garden of Dean Riddle, Phoenicia, NY.

Suppliers

Fabrics

In addition to the following specialty fabric sources, do check your local fabric stores or sewing center for cottons and linens to make into tablecloths, napkins, and seat and pillow covers.

Calico Corners
203 Gale Lane
Kennett Square, PA 19348
800-213-6366
www.calicocorners.com
Over 100 retail outlets that discount top-quality fabrics; also selected seconds. Custom workroom services available. Mail order. Catalog.

Calvin Klein Home
654 Madison Avenue
New York, NY 10022
212-292-9000
Out of New York call 800-294-7978 for a store in your area. Pure and simple linens and china of the finest quality and cleanest lines. Mail order. No catalog.

Laura Ashley
Call 800-367-2000 or visit www.lauraashley.com for a retailer near you. English-garden-look floral, stripe, check, and solid cotton fabrics in a terrific range of colors. Mail order. Catalog.

Oppenheim's
P.O. Box 29
120 East Main Street
North Manchester
IN 46962-0052
800-461-6728
Country prints, mill remnants, denim, chambray. Swatches sent on request. Mail order. Catalog.

Ralph Lauren Home Collection
867 Madison Avenue
New York, NY 10021
212-606-2100
For a store in your area, call 800-377-POLO (800-377-7656).
www.ralphlauren.com
Stylish accessories, including tableware and wonderful cotton and linen fabrics by the yard. Look too for their discount outlets. Mail order. No catalog.

Rose Brand
Call for assistance:
NY 800-223-1624
LA 800-360-5056
www.rosebrand.com
Extra-wide fabrics are a specialty at this theatrical trade provider. Great prices here on muslin, canvas, scrim, and ticking. They will also seam lengths together. Mail order. Catalog.

Rue de France
78 Thomas Street
Newport, RI 02840
800-777-0998
www.ruedefrance.com
Specialties include Country French lace panels; also a selection of fabric curtains and accessories with the look of Provence. Mail order. Catalog.

Sanderson
3 Patriot Center
285 Grand Avenue
Englewood, NJ 07631
201-894-8400
www.sanderson-online.co.uk
Furnishes fabrics and linens for outdoor table and seat covers. Call for the nearest distributor.

Food

These purveyors of specialty foods will ship your order, but for a listing of food retailers and farmers' markets selling fresh local produce call your area Chamber of Commerce. For farmers' markets, also see the website listed.

Balducci's
424 Sixth Avenue
New York, NY 10011
212-673-2600
From exquisite meats and fish to gorgeous baked goods, this food market has just about anything you can think of. Mail order (including overnight delivery on perishables). Catalog includes more items than stocked in the store.

Dean & Deluca
560 Broadway
New York, NY 10012
212-226-6800
www.deananddeluca.com
A food store of epic proportions with everything from unusual fruits and vegetables out-of-season to kitchen utensils and accessories. Mail order. Catalog contains fewer items than stocked in the store.

Esperya USA
3 Westchester Plaza
Elmsford, NY 10523
877-907-2525
www.esperya.com
Italian produce—charcuterie, cheese, wine, oil, pasta, rice, and more—plus tableware and books. You can select products by Italian region. Mail order. Catalog.

Farmers' Markets
www.ams.usda.gov/farmersmarkets/map.htm
The USDA's listing of farmers' markets. Each state has a listing of markets by city.

Foods of All Nations
2121 Ivy Road
Charlottesville, VA 22903
757-333-FOOD
www.foodofallnations.com
In business for 50 years, stocking an impressive selection of the latest food products and epicurean staples from more than 300 suppliers worldwide. Mail order. Monthly catalog and newsletter.

Whole Foods Market
250 7th Avenue at 24th Street
New York, NY 10001
212-924-5969
And stores nationwide.
www.wholefoodsmarket.com
Organic supermarkets. A wide variety of produce is available.

Furniture and accessories

Anthropologie
Call 800-309-2500 for your nearest store.
www.anthropologie.com
Good selection of garden accessories, with lots of interesting flowerpots. Nationwide locations.

Bamboo Fencer
179 Boylston Street
Jamaica Plain, MA
800-775-8641
www.bamboofencer.com
They provide fencing and gates, pergolas and orchid houses—virtually any structure made of bamboo—not only across the country, but around the world. Mail order. Catalog.

Brown Jordan
8960 Gidley Street
El Monte, CA 91731
800-743-4252
www.brownjordan.com
All types of metal furniture, from stacking chairs to umbrella tables. Call for a dealer in your area. Catalog.

Charleston Gardens
61 Queen Street
Charleston, SC 29401
800-469-0118
www.charlestongardens.com
Furniture, ornaments, planters and jardinieres, lighting, garden features, and fountains.

Colonial Williamsburg
P.O. Box 3532
Williamsburg, VA 23187-3532
800-446-9240
www.colonialwilliamsburg.com
Attractive glass hurricane lamps, candlesticks, and traditional garden accessories. Mail order. Catalog.

Crate and Barrel
646 N Michigan Avenue
Chicago, IL 60611
800-996-9960
For a retailer near you, call 800-927-9202.
www.crateandbarrel.com
A wonderful source of good-value furniture and accessories, from simple white china and glass to table linens for outdoor dining. Nationwide locations. Mail order. Catalog.

Fishs Eddy
889 Broadway
New York, NY 10011
212-420-9020
Overstock supplies for great 1950s restaurant-style mugs, plates, bowls, etc. No catalog, but call with your requests and, if available, they will be mailed post haste.

Gardener's Eden
Avon Marketplace
336 W Main Street (US 44)
Avon, CT
860-677-0846
www.gardenerseden.com
Call 800-822-1214 for a mail-order catalog. Quality garden tools and accessories, from trellises to trowels.

Hold Everything
250 W 57th Street
New York, NY 10019
212-957-9313
www.holdeverything.com
Chrome and steel baskets to collect fruit, wicker picnic baskets, shed shelving, storage accessories of all sizes. Call for a location near you. Mail order. Catalog.

The Home Depot
Stores nationwide. Call 800-430-3376 for locations.
www.homedepot.com
A wide selection of lumber, outdoor furniture, and plant material at discounted prices.

Ikea
For a store near you, call 800-254-IKEA.
www.ikea.com
Scandinavian-style garden furniture at great prices, including kit furniture and stylish inexpensive folding chairs, trestle tables, benches, and other outdoor ideas. Mail order. Catalog.

Martha By Mail
P.O. Box 60060
Tampa, FL 33660-0060
800-950-7130
www.marthabymail.com
Fancy and tasteful homewares and garden items.

Palecek
P.O. Box 225
Richmond, CA 94808-0225
800-274-7730
www.palecek.com
Manufacturers of fine crafted wicker, rattan, and wooden accent furniture. Call for a dealer in your area.

Pier One Imports
For a store in your area call 800-44PIER1 (800-447-4371).
www.pier1.com
Great home accessories, outdoor ideas, and furniture. 800 locations nationwide.

Pottery Barn
P.O. Box 7044
San Francisco, CA 94120-7044
For a store near you, call 800-922-9932.
www.potterybarn.com
Moderately priced furnishing for comfortable living indoors and out: garden furniture, kitchen and glassware, candlesticks, hurricane lamps, pillows, and table linens. Nationwide locations. For a catalog call 800-922-5507.

Restoration Hardware
935 Broadway
New York, NY 10011
212-260-9479
www.restorationhardware.com
Not just hardware, some of the funkiest home furnishings, lighting, and home and garden accessories you'll find.

Shelby Williams Industries
150 Shelby Williams Drive
Morristown, TN 37813
800-SEATING
www.shelbywilliams.com
Wonderful custom-made wicker furniture with classic styling. To the trade only; call for stockists.

Smith and Hawken
35 Corte Madera Avenue
Mill Valley, CA 94941
800-940-1170
www.smithandhawken.com
A wide variety of plants, tools, ornaments, and furniture; also a large selection of natural plant repellents and gardening remedies. Nationwide locations; call for one near you. Mail order. Catalog.

Target Stores
Stores nationwide. Call 888-304-4000 for details.
www.target.com
Reasonably priced outdoor furniture—with a little flair.

Vermont Outdoor Furniture
9 Auburn Street
Barre, VT 05641
800-588-8834
www.vermontoutdoor furniture.com
Simple, beautiful wood seating, porch swings, gliders, and tables.

The Wicker Works
at Sloan Miyasoto
2 Henry Adams Street
San Francisco, CA 92109
858-490-2595
Outdoor furnishings including elegant designs in teak and wicker. Nationwide locations; call 415-970-5400 for one near you. Catalog.

Plants, seeds, and bulbs

All of the sources listed below offer catalogs and mail order. Don't overlook your local botanical garden as a source for unique and interesting plants, bulbs, and seeds as well as accurate information.

Burpee Seeds and Plants
300 Park Avenue
Warminster, PA 18991-0001
800-888-1447
www.burpee.com
One of the oldest, largest, and finest purveyors of plants and seeds. Mail order. Large catalog.

Jackson & Perkins
P.O. Box 1028
Medford, OR 97501
800-872-7673
www.jackson-perkins.com
Roses of all sorts, all colors, and all beautiful. Mail order. Comprehensive color catalog.

Johnny's Selected Seeds
305 Foss Hill Road
Albion, ME 04910-9731
207-437-4301
www.johnnyseeds.com
Heirloom and unusual vegetables, such as tomatoes in purple, orange, and yellow. Also a wide variety of herbs and flowers. Mail order. Catalog.

Old House Gardens
536 Third Street
Ann Arbor, MI 48103-4957
734-995-1486
www.oldhousegardens.com
Antique-type flower bulbs and tubers to fill the garden with color spring, summer, and fall. Mail order only. Catalog.

Park Seed Company
1 Parkton Avenue
Greenwood, SC 29647-0001
864-941-4480
www.parkseed.com
One of the oldest, largest, and most extensive seed collections in the States. Mail order. Catalog.

John Scheepers
P.O. Box 700
Bantam, CT 06750
860-567-0838
www.johnscheepers.com
All types of bulbs, with a specialty in narcissus, including a mix of the most fragrant. A distinguished selection of amaryllis is also available. Mail order. Catalog.

Select Seeds Antique Flowers
180 Stickney Road
Union, CT 06076-4617
860-684-9310
www.selectseeds.com
Flower seed and plant specialties include old-fashioned English country-garden border flowers and antique-type fragrant, blooming vines. Mail order. Catalog.

Shady Oaks Nursery
1101 South 10th Street
P.O. Box 708
Waseca, MN 56093
800-504-8006
www.shadyoaks.com
Specialists in all types of plants for shady areas. Mail order. Catalog.

Shepherd's Garden Seeds
30 Irene Street
Torrington, CT 06790-6658
860-482-3638
www.shepherdseeds.com
Offers a wide spectrum of flower and vegetable seeds. Mail order. Catalog.

The Thyme Garden
20546 Alsea Highway
Alsea, OR 97324
541-487-8671
www.thymegarden.com
Sixty varieties of thyme, but hundreds of other plants, including a good selection of lavenders.

Van Bourgondien Brothers
P.O. Box 1000
245 Farmingdale Road, Rt 109
Babylon, NY 11702-0598
800-622-9959
www.dutchbulbs.com
Suppliers of bulbs of all types. Mail order. Catalog.

Wayside Gardens
1 Garden Lane
Hodges, SC 29695-0001
800-845-1124
www.waysidegardens.com
A standby for all sorts of perennials, with particular emphasis on day lilies and peonies, plants, shrubs, and bulbs. Mail order. Large full-color catalog.

We-Du Nurseries
2055 Polly Spout Road
Marion, NC 28752
828-738-8300
www.we-du.com
Perennials, wildflowers, flowers, shrubs, trees, bulbs, aquatic plants, and ferns.

White Flower Farm
Route 63
P.O. Box 50
Litchfield, CT 06759-0050
860-496-9624
www.whiteflowerfarm.com
A family-owned nursery offering a wide range of ornamental plants from around the world, including container-grown roses that gain a full year of bloom, old-fashioned peonies, and a large variety of delphiniums. The chatty, informative catalog is a delight to read. Mail order.

Winterthur Museum and Gardens
100 Enterprise Place
Dover, DE 19904
800-767-0500
Unique plants and garden accessories make this a fabulous place to visit, even by catalog. Many of the unusual plants were developed in their own nurseries. Mail order. Catalog.

Gardening consultants

Ask your favorite plant nursery for help in defining your garden spaces. If they cannot help you directly, they likely will be able to suggest someone local who can. Your County Cooperative Extension Service is also a helpful resource.

Lisa Bynon
P.O. Box 897
Sag Harbor, NY 11963
631-725-4680
Uses woody evergreen plants as green walls to define garden spaces as rooms filled with white blooms. Her emphasis is on unusual textures and pale flowers.

Nancy McCabe Garden Design, Inc.
P.O. Box 447
Salisbury, CT 06068
860-824-0354
This full-service landscape designer has created everything from beautiful herb and vegetable gardens to English country-style garden borders.

Dean Riddle
P.O. Box 294
Phoenicia, NY 12464
845-688-7048
This Catskill Mountain gardener will create anything from a rooftop oasis to a charming vegetable and flower garden.

Specialty paints

While latex paint can be mixed to nearly any color and is available in a number of finishes at paint and hardware stores and home centers nationwide, the following are noteworthy for their soft, suedelike finish and unique colorations.

Fine Paints of Europe
Call 800-332-1556 for a retailer near you.
www.finepaints.com
Distributors of fine European paints, including Martha Stewart's "Aracuna" line, named for the delicately colored eggs these pretty chickens lay. The color selection is derived from natural sources such as stones, shells, leaves, and petals. Mail order.

Ralph Lauren Paints
at Ralph Lauren
867 Madison Avenue
New York, NY 10022
212-606-2100
www.ralphlauren.com
A vast collection of colors that evoke the rugged, sun-drenched outdoors, divided into themes such as Suede, River Rock, and Desert. Call for the nearest distributor. Also available from Home Depot stores.

Acknowledgments

It has been enormous fun putting together *Pure Style Outdoors*. It would not have been possible without all the hard work and support from everyone at **Ryland Peters and Small**. Special thanks go to **Jacqui Small**, **Anne Ryland**, **David Peters**, **Penny Stock**, **Zia Mattocks**, and **Janet Cato**.

Fiona Craig-McFeely and **Alice Douglas** have been superb assistants. Thanks also to **Clair Wayman**, **Jen Gilman** (our wonderfully versatile nanny), **Lynda Kay**, and **Robert Davies** for his expert help in Spain.

Together with energy, humor, and enthusiasm, photographer **Pia Tryde** has produced beautiful and descriptive images. I must also thank **Nick Pope** and **Ian Skelton** for the splendid cut-out photography.

Many thanks also to the following people who have so kindly let me photograph in their gardens: **John and Colleen Matheson**; **The Manor Gardening Society**; **Nancy McCabe**; **Dean Riddle**; **David** and **Carolyn Fuest**; **Humphrey** and **Isabelle Bowden**; **Nick** and **Hermione Tudor**; **Vanessa de Lisle**; **Karl** and **Pia Sandeman**; **Lisa Bynon** and **Mona Nehrenberg**; **Timothy Leese**; and **Robert Chance**. Special thanks to my New York friend, **Tricia Foley**, for her help, guidance, and hospitality, and to **Ellen O'Neill**, who very generously let me invade her Long Island home once more.

Big hugs for **Alastair**, **Tom**, **Georgia**, **Grace**, and my parents, **John** and **Jean**, who, once again, put up with me and the agonies and angst of creating a book.

Index